The child with down's syndrome and cerebral palsy

Margaret Selpha Amateshe

The child with down's syndrome and cerebral palsy

A case study on speech development and intervention techniques

LAP LAMBERT Academic Publishing

Impressum/Imprint (nur für Deutschland/only for Germany)
Bibliografische Information der Deutschen Nationalbibliothek: Die Deutsche Nationalbibliothek verzeichnet diese Publikation in der Deutschen Nationalbibliografie; detaillierte bibliografische Daten sind im Internet über http://dnb.d-nb.de abrufbar.
Alle in diesem Buch genannten Marken und Produktnamen unterliegen warenzeichen-, marken- oder patentrechtlichem Schutz bzw. sind Warenzeichen oder eingetragene Warenzeichen der jeweiligen Inhaber. Die Wiedergabe von Marken, Produktnamen, Gebrauchsnamen, Handelsnamen, Warenbezeichnungen u.s.w. in diesem Werk berechtigt auch ohne besondere Kennzeichnung nicht zu der Annahme, dass solche Namen im Sinne der Warenzeichen- und Markenschutzgesetzgebung als frei zu betrachten wären und daher von jedermann benutzt werden dürften.

Coverbild: www.ingimage.com

Verlag: LAP LAMBERT Academic Publishing GmbH & Co. KG
Heinrich-Böcking-Str. 6-8, 66121 Saarbrücken, Deutschland
Telefon +49 681 3720-310, Telefax +49 681 3720-3109
Email: info@lap-publishing.com

Approved by: Nairobi, Kenyatta University, Diss, 2011

Herstellung in Deutschland (siehe letzte Seite)
ISBN: 978-3-659-18489-5

Imprint (only for USA, GB)
Bibliographic information published by the Deutsche Nationalbibliothek: The Deutsche Nationalbibliothek lists this publication in the Deutsche Nationalbibliografie; detailed bibliographic data are available in the Internet at http://dnb.d-nb.de.
Any brand names and product names mentioned in this book are subject to trademark, brand or patent protection and are trademarks or registered trademarks of their respective holders. The use of brand names, product names, common names, trade names, product descriptions etc. even without a particular marking in this works is in no way to be construed to mean that such names may be regarded as unrestricted in respect of trademark and brand protection legislation and could thus be used by anyone.

Cover image: www.ingimage.com

Publisher: LAP LAMBERT Academic Publishing GmbH & Co. KG
Heinrich-Böcking-Str. 6-8, 66121 Saarbrücken, Germany
Phone +49 681 3720-310, Fax +49 681 3720-3109
Email: info@lap-publishing.com

Printed in the U.S.A.
Printed in the U.K. by (see last page)
ISBN: 978-3-659-18489-5

DEDICATION

To my parents Daniel and Emily Amateshe who inspired me to pursue this course. To my beloved friend and husband, Arnold, who made it possible for me to realise my dream and to my children, for their patience and unfailing support.

ACKNOWLEDGEMENT

This course was tedious and I owe its successful completion to great support from people who care. I am truly grateful and indebted to my three supervisors: Dr. Nyamasyo, Dr. Mwangi and Dr. Runo, who have invested their intellectual resources to ensure the successful completion of this study. They have cut an image of people who are extremely patient, understanding, resourceful and thorough. Their guidance and advice were both invaluable and enriching.

Special thanks also go to the faculty and staff of the Department of English and Linguistics, and the School of Humanities and Social Sciences of Kenyatta University for their unwavering support and encouragement.

This work would not have materialised without the emotional and financial support of my beloved Arnold. You stood by me, gave your all and moreover, shouldered family responsibility while I was pursuing this course. To my children, thank you for your perseverance during my absence. My sincere and deepest gratitude also goes to my family members who urged me on when I seemed to be slipping back. Special thanks go to my two younger brothers: to David, thank you for giving me a shoulder to lean on when the tide was so high; to Maurice, thank you for your willingness to read through my work and for offering mind opening criticisms that gave me an insight into how to appropriately tackle the analysis of the study data.

ABBREVIATIONS AND ACRONYMS

CA - Chronological Age.

CNS - Central Nervous System

CP - Cerebral Palsy.

DS -   Down Syndrome.

EMC - Educable Mentally Challenged

IQ – Intelligence Quotient

KISE - Kenya Institute of Special Education

KIE - Kenya Institute of Education

MA - Mental Age.

MH – Mental Handicap

MR - Mental Retardation

MoEST - Ministry of Education Science and Technology.

SNE - Special Needs Education.

UK - United Kingdom.

UN - United Nations.

USA – United States of America

NIDCD – National Institute on Deafness and other Communication Disorders.

OPERATIONAL DEFINITION OF TERMS

Articulation
Refers to the production of individual speech sounds. Accurate articulation involves precise movement of the articulators including the tongue, lips, alveolar ridge, velum and jaw coordinated with correct air flow and voicing.

Chronological Age (CA)
The amount of time, usually expressed in years and months that have elapsed since an individual's birth.

Cerebral Palsy (CP)
A disorder of the control of voluntary movement due to brain injury at birth or near the time of birth. The speech difficulties in CP are due to paralysis of speech muscles. CP is thus not a disease.

Disability (Impairment)
Reduced function or loss of a particular body part or organ. A disability limits the ability to perform tasks such as to see, hear or talk.

Down's syndrome (DS).
A chromosomal disorder caused by an error in cell division that results in an extra 21st chromosome. The condition leads to impairments in both cognitive ability and physical growth.

Educable Mentally Challenged (EMC)
Refers to children whose abilities are adequate for them to profit from an academically oriented curriculum. However, these children are still not ready do basic writing, reading or arithmetic when they enrol into their special schools at the age of six years.

Handicap
Refers to a problem a person with a disability or impairment encounters in interacting with the environment. A disability may pose a handicap in one environment and not in another.

Inclusive Education

This refers to schools and centres of learning and educational systems that are open to all children including those with special needs and disabilities. This kind of education asserts that all learners in a school regardless of their strengths and weaknesses become part of that school.

Insertion

A compensatory phonological process where the speakers opt to introduce extra phonemes or syllables within a word, in order to make the pronunciation of the given word easier. Vowels are commonly inserted to break consonant clusters.

Language

Refers to the expression of human communication through which knowledge, belief and behaviour can be experienced, explained and shared. This sharing is based on systematic, conventionally used signs, sounds, gestures or marks that convey understood meanings within a group or community.

Mental Age (MA)

The level of an individual's mental ability expressed in terms of the chronological ages of others. A person's mental age theoretically describes his or her level of cognitive development in comparison to other people.

Mental Retardation (MR)

Refers to an intellectual disability that affects the way individuals who have it adapt to and cope with the various environments in which they find themselves.

Neurological impairment

Refers to a condition that involves the nervous system affecting the ability to move, use, feel or control certain parts of the body.

Omission

A process that involves the loss of initial, medial or final consonant sounds and syllables in a word.

Speech production

Involves the coordinated movements of the lips, tongue, teeth, palate and respiratory system.

Special Needs Education

This is a system of education designed to meet the needs of a child who is restricted in his/her ability to follow normal school curriculum because of some handicap. In Kenya, Special Needs Education caters for people with hearing, visual, mental, physical and multiple impairment.

Special school

A school offering special services to learners with special needs.

Speech

Refers to the motor act of communicating by articulating verbal expression. It is a very complicated thing involving the physical structure of the lips, teeth, tongue, palate, throat and larynx as well as mental development and social experience.

Substitution

Refers to a case where a sound is replaced by another without reference to neighbouring sounds.

Syllable

Refers to a single phoneme or a combination of several phonemes studied in any language. In phonology, the syllable is divided into onset and rhyme. The rhyme is further divided into nucleus and coda.

Intervention Techniques

Communication skills used in the school of study and geared at promoting speech development. These include exercises such as communication on one to one, use of real objects, use of pictures, imitation among others.

LIST OF TABLES

LIST OF FIGURES

TABLE OF CONTENTS

CHAPTER ONE

1.0 INTRODUCTION

This chapter looks at the background to this study, statement of the problem, the objectives and research questions that guide the study and the assumptions made, significance, scope and limitations as far as the study is concerned.

1.1 BACKGROUND TO THE STUDY

Speech is the motor act of communicating by articulating verbal expression (Leung and Kao, 1999). According to Zattore and Gandour (2008), in order to produce speech, thoughts must be translated into linguistic representations, which are then sent to speech mechanisms that can coordinate, initiate, modify and execute the articulation of an utterance. On the other hand, language is the expression of human communication through which knowledge, beliefs and behaviour can be experienced, explained and shared. This sharing is based on systematic, conventionally used signs, sounds, gestures or marks that convey understood meanings within a group (National Institute on Deafness and other Communication Disorders; October, 2002).

Speech and language acquisition is a prerequisite to oral communication. The most intensive period of speech and language development for humans is during the first three years of life, a period when the brain is developing and maturing. These skills appear to develop best in a world that is rich with sounds, sight and consistent exposure to the speech and language of others. As the speech mechanism (jaw, lips, tongue) and voice mature, an infant is able to make controlled sounds. Normal speech progresses through stages of cooing, babbling, echolalia, jargon, words and word combinations and sentence formation (Buckley & Bird, 2001).

Children vary in their development of speech and language. There is however a natural progression or "timetable" for mastery of these skills for each language. Typically, simple skills are reached before the more complex ones can be learned. There is a general age and time when most children pass through these periods. These milestones help doctors and other professionals determine when a child may need extra help to speak (National Institute on Deafness and other Communication Disorders, April, 2001).

In general, a child is considered to have speech delay if the child's speech development is significantly below the norm for children of the same age (Honda, 2006). Studies indicate that Mental Handicap (MH) is the most common cause of speech delay, accounting for more than 50% of cases (Westling, 1986; Kumin, 1994). Children with Cerebral Palsy (CP) also experience speech delay as a result of neurological impairment, arising from the condition suffered (Levitt, 2010). Numerous brain areas are recruited in speech production and they hang in a precarious balance that is easily affected by neurological disease and dysfunction (Zattore and Gandour, 2008). This study sought to observe these two groups of children with special focus on the degree to which their conditions affect their speech development.

A number of developmental problems accompany delayed onset of speech in these children. In addition, speech delay may have a significant impact on their personal, social, academic and, later on, vocational life. Early identification and appropriate intervention may mitigate the emotional, social and cognitive deficits of this disability and may improve the outcome (Dockrell and Messer, 1999). This study sought to observe speech delay in children with DS and CP conditions in Maria Magdalena Special School and what speech techniques are used, as a form of intervention.

As a result of the many challenges facing children with DS and CP the world over, and who is the focus of this study, Special Needs Education (SNE), a system for the delivery of services to such children has been put in place. The right to inclusive education was initially stated in Salamanca Statement and Framework for Action (2000) in 1994. It emphasized that the schools need to change and adapt to the diverse needs of all learners. The UN Convention on the Rights of Persons with Disabilities (1994) established the inclusive education as a legal right (Ngigi and Macharia, 2006). This kind of education programme is customized to address each individual child's unique needs. Accommodations and modifications to the regular programme may include changes in curriculum, supplementary aides or equipment and the provision of specialized physical adaptations that allow children to participate in the environment to the fullest extent possible (McBrayer & Lian, 2002). According to Howard (1996) the philosophy of inclusion hinges on making the learners such as those with DS and CP conditions, and teachers to become better members of the community and to create new visions for community and schools.

In Kenya, SNE caters for people with hearing, visual, mental, physical and multiple impairments (MoEST, 1994). This study sought to observe children with mental and physical impairment as a result of DS and CP respectively. This is guided by the fact that DS affects the mental state whereas CP affects the physical state of a person. The provision of education and training to all Kenyans is fundamental to government overall development strategy (MoEST, 2004). This has led to the establishment of the Kenya Institute of Special Education (KISE) in 1986 and departments of special education at Kenyatta (1995) and Maseno (1997) universities respectively. However, Ndurumo (1993) points out that special schools and units have existed in Kenya since before independence, among them, Jacaranda School for the Mentally Handicapped and the Aga Khan Special School.

Through the provision of specialized training, the MoEST hopes to facilitate provision of effective and efficient professional and support services to learners with DS and CP in institutions of learning (Ministry of Education Special Needs Policy, 2009). According to Bricker and Schiefelbush (1984), children with special needs, and in the case of this study those with DS and CP, require teachers who are sensitive and responsive to student-initiated communication(s) as they occur in daily interactions. Such spontaneous and natural interactions will affect the social and communicative behaviour of the student and can easily be incorporated within an instructional framework.

This study focused on Maria Magdalena Special School for children with Mental Handicap (MH) in Thika Municipality Division. This is largely a boarding primary school with a few commuters, which was established in 1992 under MoEST and the sponsorship of the Catholic Church, with the aim of assisting children and young adults with disabilities, after a needs assessment research carried out in the location. It has a seven class system namely: Nursery class (Age 9-12), Pre-Primary (Age10-13), Primary one (Age12-15), Primary two (Age14-16), Primary three (Age15-16), Pre-vocational (Age17-19) and vocational class (Age19-25). The classification of the children is based on their age and the skills mastered in class. The school has a total of 90 students and 13 teachers.

The study sought to describe the nature of speech handicap in children with DS and CP. It also posed the question: to what extent do the speech intervention techniques used by teachers enhance speech development in these two categories of children?

1.2 STATEMENT OF THE PROBLEM
Existing academic studies related to children with mental and physical handicap in Kenya outline what needs to be done, in order to fully incorporate them in society. For instance, Oswago (2005) examines the lexical density found in the spoken language of children with Mental Handicap and the unique characteristics of this language. The study plays a pivotal role in highlighting the strengths of children with MH in relation to

language skills. However, the study fails to address the minimal or lack of speech in children with DS and CP and who are capable of developing this skill if trained. The focus of the study is on those who already can produce speech.

It has been noted, therefore, that studies have not been done on ways of developing and improving speech in children with DS and CP. The literature that exists on the same (Elsenson and Ogilvie, 1963; Bloodstein, 1984; Chapman, 1997; Hassold and Patterson, 1998) is by authors from the West. What the MoEST in Kenya outlines is relevant although inadequate in relation to the adverse speech defects of children with DS and CP. Consequently, there is inadequate information that could be used in the planning and implementation of techniques for enhancing development of speech in such children in Kenya. This study, therefore, set out to examine speech development in children with DS and CP and the speech-related intervention techniques used, with the intention of enhancing development of speech among such children.

1.3 OBJECTIVES OF THE STUDY
The study was guided by the following objectives:
1. To establish the speech ability of children with DS and CP at the time of the study.
2. To establish the relationship between the chronological age (CA) of these children and speech development.
3. To describe the speech intervention techniques employed by teachers in order to enhance the development of speech in children with DS and CP.

1.4 RESEARCH QUESTIONS
The study was guided by the following research questions:
1. What is the speech ability of children with DS and CP at the time of this study?

2. What is the relationship between the CA of these children and their speech development?

3. What speech intervention techniques do teachers employ to enhance the development of their speech?

1.5 RESEARCH ASSUMPTIONS

The research made the following assumptions:

1. With training, children with DS and CP have the potential for speech development.

2. There exists a relationship between the CA of these children and speech development.

3. There are speech intervention techniques employed by teachers to enable children with DS and CP develop speech at different levels.

1.6 SIGNIFICANCE OF THE STUDY

Masakhwe (The Saturday Standard 24, 2009) reiterates that children with disabilities, in the case of this study, children with DS and CP, face many education obstacles. Solutions to these impediments should top the priority list of education planners and administrators. There is considerable evidence to indicate that such can profit extensively by proper training presented with patience and understanding.

It is therefore anticipated that the findings of this study will yield information for use by teachers in charge of children with DS and CP, so that they too can use similar speech intervention techniques to enhance speech among these children. Linguists too may use the findings of this study to document speech development techniques, which can be used by speech therapists to support children with DS and CP. Parents with such children will also be able to appreciate their speech problems and support them in developing it using similar techniques.

The findings of this study should provide useful insight to policy makers, curriculum developers and educationists such as the MoEST, Kenya Institute of Education (KIE) and Kenya Institute of Special Education (KISE) to develop appropriate policy, curriculum, and teacher training programmes and establish relevant learning facilities that will promote speech development among children with DS and CP in Kenya. It is hoped that the findings of this study will augment, supplement or add on to the existing branch of human knowledge in the area of speech delay in children with DS and CP and intervention techniques used to promote it. It is also hoped that this study will serve as a basis for further research in this area, since there is a lot that needs to be done to improve the lives and education of children with DS and CP.

1.7   SCOPE AND LIMITATIONS

This study dealt with speech development in children with DS and CP. Although there are various categories of children with special needs in Kenya, the study limited itself to children with DS and CP who are able to attend school and learn speech for communication. There are many causes of speech delay in children. However, this study specifically looked at speech delay as a result of mental handicap and neurological impairment, which falls under physical handicap and is caused by cerebral palsy. Although speech and Language go together, this study touched on the aspect of speech.

Bloodstein (1984) states that children with DS and CP basically speak in sounds, words, and simpler and shorter sentences. The study therefore limited itself to observing and analyzing linguistic data covering these three areas, as produced by the sampled children after the techniques had been employed. The data was recorded in the English and Kiswahili since these are the language the children are exposed to.

Although there are many schools in Kenya catering for children with DS and CP, the study limited itself to Maria Magdalena Special School for Children with Mental Handicap in Thika, purposively sampled due to its multi-ethnic outlook. Besides, most of the children with DS and CP in the school have mild to moderate conditions, a fact that makes them suitable for this study. The school has a total of seven classes. However, the study focused on five classes namely: the Nursery, Pre-Primary, Primary one, Primary two and Primary three classes, purposively sampled to reflect the cumulative phases of the intervention techniques.

The school of study has three main categories of children with special needs namely: children with CP, children with DS and children with Autism. However, the study looked at only two: those with "Down Syndrome" (DS) and those with "Cerebral Palsy" (CP). This is because they had the defining speech characteristics that the research sought to address. Besides, dealing with all the three categories would have made this study too broad.

Summary of the chapter

In this chapter, the preliminaries that shape up this study are presented. Next, the study looks at the review of the works related to the present study and the theoretical framework that has models that will help interpret and analyze the data of this study.

CHAPTER TWO

2.0 LITERATURE REVIEW AND THEORETICAL FRAMEWORK

2.1 INTRODUCTION

This chapter deals with the review of the works related to the present study. The chapter is divided into four sub-sections: studies on normal speech and language development in children, studies on children with mental and physical handicap, speech development in children with DS, speech development in children with CP, literature on speech intervention techniques and the morphological and syllable structure of Kiswahili and English. The chapter ends with the theoretical framework which has models that helped interpret and analyse the data of this study.

2.2 REVIEW OF RELATED LITERATURE

2.2.1 Normal Speech and Language Development in Children.

Children vary in their development of speech and Language. According to Leung and Kao (1999), to determine whether a child has speech delay, there is need to have basic knowledge of speech milestones. Normal speech progresses through stages of cooing, babbling, echolalia, jargon, words and word combinations and sentence formation. The milestones are identifiable skills that can serve as a guide to normal development (Schwartz, 1996).

Beginning signs of communication occur in the first few days of life, when an infant learns that a cry will bring food, comfort and companionship (Schoenstadt, 2006). According to Maneno and Runo (2007), both the sounds of comfort and distress provide the infant with the exercise needed to develop the complex muscles required for speech. As the speech mechanism (jaw, lips, tongue and throat) and voice mature, an infant is able to make controlled sounds. This begins in the first few months of life with 'cooing', a quiet pleasant, repetitive vocalization (Schoenstadt, 2006). The 'coos' and 'girgles' of the infant are the beginnings of language and speech development and production

(Maneno and Runo, 2007). The child's random babbling gradually begins to take form as if the child were practicing consonant (*baba, papa*) and vowel (*woo, iiii*) sounds.

Maneno and Runo (2007) assert that in the first months of life, the infant shows a startle response to sharp noises. At 3 to 6 months, the infant begins to show an interest in sounds, plays with saliva and responds to voices. For example, loud shouts will make the infant literally scream but a calm and soothing voice will make a crying infant stop and be attentive. During the next 3 to 6 months, infants begin to babble, emitting such sounds as "goo-goo" and "ga-ga". The start of babbling is determined mainly by biological maturation and not reinforcement, hearing, caregiver or parent infant interaction. It is amazing to note that even deaf babies babble for a time. Babbling soon turns into a type of nonsense speech called jargon that often has the tone and cadence of human speech but does not contain real words.

At approximately 6 to 9 months, the infants begin to understand their first words (vocabulary) while their receptive vocabulary begins to develop in the second half of the first year. Its growth increases dramatically in the second year from an average of 12 words understood at the first birthday (words like *kuja-come, washa-light, hiyo-that one, mama-mother, baba-father*). By the time the infant is 2 years, he or she has an estimated capacity of 300 words or more which he or she actually understands.

According to Schwartz (1996), at approximately 9-12 months, infants begin to understand phrases such as when asked to say "bye-bye". Infants utter their first words at about 10-15 months of age. The infant's spoken vocabulary rapidly increase once the first word is spoken (such as *mama-mother, pusi-cat, gari- car*) reaching an average of 200 to 275 words by the age of 2. By the time children are 18-24 months of age they usually utter two word statements such as 'more milk'. During this two-word stage, children rapidly learn that words symbolize objects, actions and thoughts. They quickly grasp the importance of expressing concepts and of the role that language plays in communicating with others (Maneno and Runo, 2007; Schwartz, 1996).

To convey meaning with two-word utterances, the child relies heavily on gesture, tone and content. Maneno and Runo (2007) state that at around 18 months of age, children experience a surge in vocabulary growth and rather than learning one new word a week, they learn several words and phrases in a day such as "see doggie", "book there", "more milk", "big car", "mama walk" among others. The most intensive period of speech and language development is during the first three years of life, a period when the brain is developing and maturing. These skills appear to develop best in a world that is rich with sounds, sights and consistent exposure to the speech and language of others (Piaget, 1969; Drew and Hardman, 2000)

At ages 3 to 4, a child's vocabulary rapidly increases and he/she begins to master the rules of language such as phonology, morphology, syntax, semantics and pragmatics (Schoenstadt, 2006). For instance, the child is able to use the following: plurals and past tense, knows age and sex, can count up to three objects, asks questions, tells stories and relates experiences. At ages 4 to 5, the child is able to use six to eight words per sentence, names four colours and counts 10 pennies (Schoenstadt, 2006).

Schwartz (1996) states that by the time the child is 5 years of age, approximately 90% of his/her utterances will be intelligible to unfamiliar adults. Most studies carried out confirm the fact that children will have mastered the syntax of their first language by the age of 5 years (Nyamasyo, 1985; Ndung'u, 1991). However, this is not the case in children with DS and CP. Studies have established that they lag behind significantly in the development of their speech (Peacock, 2000; Oelwein, 1995). According to Leung and Kao (1999), a child is considered to have speech delay if the child's speech development is significantly below the norm for children of the same age. This study set out to observe the speech development in children with DS and CP. The purpose was to establish whether their speech lagged behind their chronological age (CA) compared to their normally developing peers, and as indicated by various studies.

2.2.2 Studies on Children with Mental and Physical Handicap

Mental Retardation (MR) is a generalized disorder characterised by significantly impaired cognitive functioning and deficits in two or more adaptive behaviours with onset before the age of 18. MR is a disability and not a disease (Ianneli, 2005; Kiarie, 2006). According to Berne-Smith, Patton and Kim (2006), DS is the best known biologically caused condition associated with MR and developmental disabilities. This study sought to observe children with DS, with the purpose of establishing to what extent the condition affected the development of their speech.

According to Finnie (2004), people nowadays prefer not to use the label "mental retardation" but rather talk about mild, moderate or severe learning disorders. Similarly, Iannelli (2005) points out that the long used term MR has acquired an undesirable social stigma. As a result of this stigma, doctors and health care practitioners have begun replacing it with the term Intellectual Disability (ID). Although this study recognizes the fact that MR is a biological term which is frequently used in text books, it used the equivalent term 'Mental Handicap' (MH) due to the two arguments presented above.

Heward (1996) states that the causes of MR can be prenatal, perinatal or postnatal. All of these etiologic factors associated with MR can be classified as either organic (biological or medical) or environmental. For the majority of individuals with MR, however, the exact cause is unknown. Ianneli (2005) states that there are four categories of MR as classified by Intelligence Quotient (IQ) score: mild, moderate, severe and profound. Children with mild MR may experience substantial performance deficits only in school. Their social and communication skills may be normal or nearly so. They are likely to become independent or semi-independent adults. Most children with moderate MR show significant developmental delays during their pre-school years. On the other hand, most persons with severe and profound MR are identified in infancy. Some adults with this condition can be semi-independent. Others need 24 hour support throughout their lives. This study sought to observe children with MH who are mildly to moderately handicapped since they exhibit speech characteristics that meet the objectives of the study.

Associated with retarded mental development is the delay in the onset of speech. The use of single words occurs at a later age (Pruthi, 1994). This stage of speech development may persist with minimal growth in vocabulary for several years with late onset of the use of phrases. According to Heward (1996), these phrases may be used in incomplete form for a long period. The majority are never used adequately. Shriver (2010) points out that for children with MH learning will take longer, require more repetition and skills, and may need to be adapted to their learning level. Nevertheless, virtually every child is able to learn and become a participating member of the community. This study sought to establish the relationship between the CA of children with MH who have mild to moderate conditions and their speech development, a milestone it is assumed they lag in.

According to Heward (1996), children with **physical impairment** are an extremely varied population. Their physical disabilities may be mild, moderate or severe. Their intellectual functioning may be normal, below normal or above normal. These children may have a single impairment or a combination of impairments. Physical disability may be described as Orthopaedic or Neurological (Heward, 1996; Ndurumo, 1993). The former involves the skeletal system – bones, joints, limbs and associated muscles while the latter involves the nervous system affecting the ability to move, use, feel or control certain parts of the body. Orthopaedic and neurological impairment are two distinct and separate types of disabilities but they may cause similar limitations in movement. This study focused on Cerebral Palsy condition that is the cause of neurological impairment, resulting in speech delay in children with CP.

Cerebral palsy is one of the most prevalent causes of physical impairment in children of school age. It is a long-term condition resulting from a lesion to the brain or an abnormality of brain growth that causes a variety of disorders of movement of posture (Ndurumo, 1993). Children with CP, the group this study seeks to observe, have disturbances of voluntary motor functions that may include paralysis, extreme weakness, and lack of coordination, involuntary convulsions and other motor disorders. They may have little or no control over their arms, legs or speech, depending on the type and degree of impairment. They may also have impaired vision or hearing (Heward, 1996).

Intellectual impairments may accompany Cerebral palsy. Heward (1996) found that 41% of the children with CP in their study scored below 70 on a standardized test. Smith (1984) affirms that the probability of MR appears greater when a convulsive disorder is also present. According to Ndurumo (1993), children with CP, some of whom have brain damage, are frequently found to be performing in the MR range when assessed.

However, Ndurumo (1993) warns that the 70% figure should be interpreted cautiously because of the problems inherent in testing children with CP. They state that intelligence tests have both verbal and performance tests yet children with CP have speech problems and motor coordination difficulties. They would undoubtedly be expected to perform poorly in intelligence tests where the manipulation of objects is required. Thus, an IQ score should never serve as the sole descriptor of a child's actual or potential ability. This study sought to establish, using background information, whether children with CP in Maria Magdalena Special School have both physical and mental handicap and to what degree their physical handicap or both, affected their speech development.

2.2.3   Speech development in children with Down's syndrome

Ainsworth and Baker (2004) claim that DS is the congenital form of retardation associated with intellectual disability where the diagnosis can be made shortly after birth. It is a chromosomal disorder caused by an error in cell division that results in the presence of an additional third chromosome 21 or 'trisomy 21' (Crane, 2002). Most people with DS exhibit moderate to severe retardation with an IQ of below 50 compared to normal children with an IQ of 100, while motor development and coordination are nearly always affected (Selikowitz, 1997).

According to Ainsworth and Baker (2004), mental development usually proceeds relatively normally from birth to about six months of age. However, by age one year, IQ scores begin to drift gradually downward to about 30. Mental capacity of children with DS is almost always approximately that of 4 or 5 year old normally developing children (Rondal, 1995). However, Dockrell and Messer (1999) state that although it used to be thought these children would not progress beyond a Mental Age (MA) of 4 to 5 years, there is increasing evidence that some individuals can achieve much more than was originally thought. Buckley and Bird (2001) state that speech difficulties hold back the children's ability to talk and to develop grammar. According to Rondal (1995), the onset of meaningful speech (one word utterance) is delayed and may appear at 24-30 months of age. This study sought to establish the age at which children with DS develop speech and whether it developed beyond the 4 or 5 year level that some studies indicate as the limit.

Pruthi (1994) notes that children with DS use simpler and shorter sentences as compared to normal children. Most such children fail to acquire complex grammatical constructions such as correct use of complex questions. However, Cichetti and Beeghly (1990) point out that the cognitive problems that are found among such children can also be found among typical children. Deficits in motor coordination and timing adversely affect the speech production system. Children with DS show a deficit in developing and utilizing programmed motor sequences (Rondal, 1995). This study sought to assess the speech ability of these children in relation to the type of structures they produced.

Although some of the physical genetic limitations of children with DS cannot be overcome, education and proper care will improve the quality of life. Developing of speech and language abilities may take longer but finally these children do develop the communication skills they need. According to Shriver (2010), children with DS have a wide range of abilities and talents and each child develops at his or her own particular pace. They should be given the opportunity and encouragement to develop their talents and gifts. It may take them longer than other children to reach developed mental milestones, but many of these milestones will eventually be met.

2.2.4   Speech development in children with CP

CP may be described as a group of conditions, usually originating in childhood and characterized by paralysis, weakness, and lack of coordination of the skeletal or speech related muscles, or any other aberration of the motor control centre of the brain. In addition to such motor dysfunction, CP may include learning difficulties, psychological problems, sensory defects and convulsive behaviour of organic origin. (Ndurumo, 1993; Levitt, 2010). CP, which is a non-progressive condition, affects the developing brain. It usually occurs before, during or shortly after birth. This accounts for 90% of all the CP cases. It also may occur in early childhood. This accounts for about 10% of all the CP cases (Peacock, 2000). In developing countries, CP is the leading cause of physical disability while in Kenya; it is the second major cause (Levitt, 2010).

According to Finnie (2004), about half the population of CP children will have moderate or severe learning disorders. Bjorklund (2007) points out that cerebral palsy and mental retardation are two different disabilities. The same person may or may not have both. Most people with CP have normal intelligence. However, they may also have additional problems such as seizures, mental retardation or other learning disabilities, vision or hearing loss. Cerebral palsy is a life-long condition. Once the brain has been damaged, it cannot repair itself (Peacock, 2000). This study set out to observe children with CP with an intention of establishing to what degree their physical or/and mental handicap affected their speech development.

The speech production for communication is often affected in children with CP (Hong, 2007). According to Plante (2004), if the condition is severe, the affected child enjoys few normal developmental experiences and a marked delay in speech. Some children have a lot of difficulty moving the muscles that control the sound making operation. The length of vocalizations is generally short, due to lack of breath support. Damage to the neuromuscular sites involved in the execution of speech movements may affect strength and timing of muscles contraction (Dancie, 2009).

Caruso and Strand (1999) state that the muscles of the chest wall (rib cage, diaphragm, abdomen) larynx, pharynx, soft palate, tongue, jaw and lips act under the control of the nervous system to produce the air pressures and flows that are transformed to the sounds of speech. The muscles of the chest wall regulate speech breathing to provide a quick inspiration and then sustain a sufficient and relatively constant air pressure in the lungs as air is expired during a spoken breath. The motor dysfunction accompanying CP can seriously impede the ability to produce intelligible speech (Berne-Smith et al, 2006) since it affects the muscles responsible for speech production. Such children are not able to carry out coordinative movements of the respiratory, laryngeal and oral muscles for articulation. The result of the above malfunctions is delayed speech. This study observed the speech delay in children with CP with the intention of establishing how the effect to the speech muscles impedes speech development.

2.2.5   Literature on speech intervention techniques

Speech delay may have a significant impact on personal, academic and later on, vocational life. Early identification and appropriate intervention may mitigate the emotional, social and cognitive deficits of the disability and may improve the outcome (McBrayer and Lian, 2002). The management of a child with speech delay should be individualized. Teachers should consider the use of small group instruction (Hassold and Patterson, 1998).

To realize their objectives, teachers are required to use task-analysis in which they break learning tasks into smaller sequential skills which they systematically teach to the children with DS and CP, until they master them (Mutua and Dimitrov, 2001). Once the child has mastered one step, the next is introduced. This ensures that the children are not overwhelmed. According to Reynold and Dombeck (2006), verbal directions and abstract lectures are not effective methods for teaching children with MH. They do better in environments where visual aides such as charts, pictures and graphs are used as much as possible. Such visual components are useful for helping learners to understand what is expected of them. Piaget (1969) notes that cognitive capacities unfold naturally. However, this is not the case for children with DS and CP. There is need for the instructors to draw upon the environment to influence the development of cognitive skills. That mental development progresses as a result of children's interactions with the surroundings.

The teacher must remember that when dealing with children, speech training can and should be fun. Much of it must be indirectly motivated in the form of games and other teaching devices. No progress in speech training can be made unless the teacher is able to secure a satisfactory response from the child. In order to accomplish this, a rather high level of interest and morale must be maintained (Anderson and Newby, 1973). This study sought to establish whether similarly, the speech techniques used at Maria

Magdalena Special School involved the use of an environment that employed a variety of visual aides that provided fun and motivation to the learner, consequently, enhancing speech development.

The Ministry of Education in Kenya also suggests intervention strategies that are fun to the Learner. According to Kiarie (2006), other instructional considerations are recommended in a guide book on handling students with special needs published by the Kenya Ministry of Education (1995).They include: modeling drills and practice to promote over-learning, attention to relevance and applicability to the students' lives, short learning activities, generous use of prompts and rewards, use of concrete materials as much as possible, use of visuals to promote understanding of concepts and explicit teaching of such self-care skills as toileting, dressing and grooming.

Bloodstein (1984) points out that in order to facilitate the onset of or improve speech, children with CP for example, will need exercises to strengthen the breathing musculature and practice speaking with deeper inspirations and longer, more controlled expiration. Learning to relax the tight spasm of the laryngeal musculature may help to produce a less hoarse or intermittently breathy voice quality. Equally important is practice in control of adduction and abduction of the vocal cords for articulation of voiced and voiceless sounds. Muscular exercise is necessary for increasing the strength and motility of the organs of articulation. For example, work on the tongue in children with DS may include relaxation exercises in which the child allows the organ to be manipulated, and strengthening exercises in which the child attempts to move it in different directions against increasing amounts of resistance (Elsenson and Ogilvie, 1963). Similar exercises may be used for the lips, jaws and velum. Special practice should be given in movements that are critical for speech, such as approximation of the lips, elevation of the tongue to the roof of the mouth, and velopharyngeal closure.

This study observed children with DS and CP who lack or possess minimal speech, and assessed how far the speech intervention techniques employed assisted them to articulate sounds, words, and sentences that initially had been elusive to them. The study focused on the way the techniques used assisted each individual child to develop strength, relaxation and control of the various parts of the speech organs, resulting in speech development and production. The success of these techniques was marked by the attainment of this linguistic milestone by these children, however minimal.

In teaching trainable children to talk, the goal must be good usable speech. Not useful speech (Molloy, 1965). In the case of this study, the success of speech intervention techniques used were measured against the ability of the initially mute children to produce sounds, those with sounds to graduate to words and finally to sentences. If finally they are able to communicate their thoughts and basic needs, they are termed successful, bearing in mind their handicapping conditions.

2.2.6 Kiswahili morphology system and syllable structure

This study found it necessary to briefly describe the morphological system and syllable structure of Kiswahili, since a greater percentage of the data in this study was collected in the same language before being translated into English. In the preceding chapter under scope and limitations, it was indicated that the two languages would be used in the collection of data (Ref. Ch. 1; p.9). It was noted that the children accessed in this study found it a lot easier to pronounce words, phrases and sentences in Kiswahili as opposed to English, as is illustrated in chapter four under presentation and analysis of data. This is because Kiswahili is the language the children are frequently exposed to, being the main mode of instruction in the school.

2.2.6.1 Kiswahili morphological system

The morphological system and syntax of Kiswahili are very closely related since the syntactic arrangement is based on morphology. Just like English, it has derivational and inflectional morphology. According to Mbaabu (1992), most words have roots and structurally, word formation processes. Kiswahili, being a Bantu language, is agglutinative with a small inflective element. Below is an illustration:

Anasoma (She/he is reading)

Mtoto anasoma (The child is reading)

In the examples above, the word **'Anasoma'** is a complete sentence, with the subject and verb glued together. The subject prefix can also co-occur with a noun subject as shown in the second example. Noun classes are morphologically arranged. The presence of the nominal classification system governs word formation, all grammatical correlations and the syntactic structure of sentences, all the members of which must be unified in morphological and syntactical correspondences (Mathooko and Mudhune, 2004). Below is an illustration:

A-WA Class

Mtoto huyu mtukutu anacheza (This naughty child is playing)

Watoto hawa watukutu wanacheza (These naughty children are playing)

Nouns are divided into classes by logical correlation. Thus, we have the class of objects, human beings, animals, and so on. Kiswahili has altogether fifteen classes. The **'A-WA'** class illustrated above comes first in the nominal class system and deals with living things (Okumu, 2006). Note that the system of nominal classification affects the whole of Kiswahili grammatical structure as shown in the example above. It is used to express singularity and plurality, animation and non animation, and the quantitative categories. Knowledge of the Kiswahili morphology system made it possible for this study to analyse the complete and defective structures of the speech of children with DS and CP.

It also guided the study in analysing the syntactic structures of the respondents using Halliday's (1985) Systemic Theory.

2.2.6.2 Kiswahili and English syllable structure

Syllable structure affects the relative distribution of consonants and vowels within a word. Kiswahili has an open syllable system (CV) as opposed to a closed one (CVC) found in English. For example, the word **'Kiti'** for **'Chair'** as observed in the study data has an open syllable system. This also applies to borrowed words such as **'televisheni'** for **'television'**. Although the borrowed words may have the English 'consonant vowel consonant' (CVC) structure, when used in Kiswahili, they always must end with a vowel as illustrated above.

Mbaabu (1992) states that virtually, every letter in a Kiswahili word is pronounced and every letter (or letter combination) corresponds to only one Kiswahili sound as in **"dirisha'** (Window), a word observed in the study data. Where we have consonant cluster in a word, it is assumed that there is a vowel separating them, although absent orthographically. For instance, it is assumed that the word **'daktari'** has a high front short vowel / i / between the voiceless velar plosive / k / and the voiceless alveolar plosive / t /. In Kiswahili, all the nasal sounds have syllabic status and are therefore referred to as syllabic consonants. That is, they are considered independent syllables and are not linked to other sounds that precede or come after them. For example, the word 'Mwalimu' (teacher) in the study data can be divided into four syllables namely: **m.wa.li.mu.** The initial syllable 'm' has syllabic status since it is a nasal consonant. Understanding the Kiswahili syllable structure was important in analysing the data of this study especially where phonological processes such as omission occurred in the speech of the respondents.

In English on the other hand, the syllable is an essential unit in the analysis of the word and other prosodic features. The syllable can be defined both phonetically and phonologically. As a phonetic unit, it has the onset and the rhyme in its structure to describe it. The rhyme is further divided into nucleus and coda. However, this study did not address the phonetic description of the syllable but the phonological one.

Phonologically, the syllable gives the basis for organizing and expressing constraints on possible phoneme sequences such as omission/deletion, insertion, substitution and coalescence. Phonological processes, which are assimilatory and non-assimilatory in nature, are related to structural and physiological aspects of speech production (Massamba, 1996). This study, in analyzing the speech ability of the respondents, made reference to such phonological processes as was observed in the data collected. Special attention was paid to how children with DS and CP, produce the speech they have developed and how their condition interferes with this production resulting in omissions, substitution and insertion.

2.3 THEORETICAL FRAMEWORK
2.3.1 INTRODUCTION
Beirne-Smith et al (2006) states that the development of speech is a complicated and fascinating process that is only partially understood. Given the complexities involved in speech development, especially among children with DS and CP, this study adopted an eclectic theoretical approach. The study therefore concentrated on, but did not limit itself to three theoretical frameworks: Cognitive Development Theory, Motor Theory, and Systemic Theory.

2.3.2 Theory of Cognitive Development

As cited by Orodho (2004), cognitive development is that aspect of development that deals with thinking, problem solving, intelligence and language (Black and Pucket, 1996). The original tenets of Cognitive Development Theory were formulated by Jean Piaget, based on observations of his own (normal) children. He viewed mental development as a result of the continuous interaction with and adaptation to the environment or the child's perception of it.

According to Piaget (1969), each child progresses through stages of development in which various cognitive skills are acquired. Cognitive growth occurs in a series of invariant and independent stages. The child's ability to think and learn changes with age as the child matures. The sensorimotor stage is characterized by sensory experiences and motor activity. As young children become more aware of the surrounding environment, they begin to distinguish between themselves and other persons and objects. The second stage, preoperational, involves more than purely physical operations. Children begin to use symbols for the people and objects around them, assimilate customs and acquire new experiences by imitating the actions of others.

During the concrete operations stage, children develop further abilities to order and classify objects. Although their mental operations are more highly developed, children are usually limited to solving problems with which they have direct or concrete experience. The ability to perform abstract thinking and reason by hypothesis is said to develop around the chronological age of 11 or 12years, and characterizes the formal operations or abstract stage.

It was Piaget's contention that although different children progress through various stages at different rates, the sequence is the same. He provides an interesting framework from which to view cognitive development in children with mental challenge. According to Beirne - Smith et al (2006), Piaget's theory has been applied to children with mental handicap by Inhelder (1968) and Woodward (1963, 1979), who view these children as progressing through the same stages of cognitive development as their typically developing peers, with the major differences in rate and highest level achieved. The age at which a child who is mentally handicapped will reach each stage will be later than the normal child and

the more severe the retardation, the slower the progression through the stage of development. Children with mental handicap often have cognitive structures more typical of chronologically younger children.

According to Inhelder (1968), children who are mildly mentally retarded may reach the concrete operations level but individuals who have been called moderately retarded will go no further than the preoperational stage. Those who are severely or profoundly retarded will remain at the sensorimotor level, a stage characterized by sensory experiences and motor activity.

From Piaget's perspective, mental development progresses as a result of children's interactions with the surroundings. The educator's role therefore is that of a provider of materials and opportunities appropriate to children's stage of developmental sequence to determine a child's readiness for a particular task, to consider the rate and the expected optimal levels of functioning when planning curricula for children with varying levels of mental challenge. This view of cognitive development appears to have important implications for teaching children with DS and CP, because education should present an environment that stimulates development of maximum potential (Drew and Hardman, 2000).

The theory was used to account for the fact that the speech of children with DS and CP failed to progress normally through all the stages and that, they hardly developed more complex language skills. The theory was also used to explain lack of speech development in these children and the need for specific speech intervention techniques by educators to help develop it. The theory helped the study to assess the techniques used in Maria Magdalena Special School to facilitate development of speech. The study sought to find out at what level various tasks were introduced to help each individual learner develop speech and if these tasks presented an environment that stimulated development of maximum potential.

2.3.3 Motor Theory

Although the controls of speech are sensory; that is, auditory, visual, tactile and kinesthetic, the production of speech is a neuromuscular process and as such, is as dependent upon motor skills as is any other mechanical ability. Therefore, the motor development of children is an important factor in determining the age at which they will begin to talk as well as the rate of their speech learning and the quality of their articulation at any given period (Anderson and Newby, 1973).

According to Ladefoged (1982), the proponent of the Motor Theory, all speech is the product of motor behaviour-muscular movement of the vocal organs. He explains the phenomenon of motor equivalence in terms of what are called **coordinate structure-physiological systems** that act together to produce the required effects. Thus, we can think of the variations in sub-glottal pressure that occur during an utterance as the products of a coordinative structure consisting of the lungs, the sensory systems that supply the brain with information about the state of the lungs (for example whether they are expanded or whether they have very little air in them), the muscles involved in adjusting positions of the rib cage and the diaphragm and the central processes relating all these.

The sub-glottal pressure that can be produced at any given moment is constrained by this coordinative structure. For example, the control of the position of the lower lip depends on a coordinative structure involving the lip muscles and the muscles fixing the position of the lower jaw and on information on the state of these and other factors including the movements of the upper lip. In speech motor planning stage, motor goals are specified to formulate action strategies for example, close lips and raise soft palate for /b/ in 'boy'.

This study used the Motor theory to explain the absence of speech in children with DS and CP due to lack of coordination of the speech organs. The theory was also used to explain why children with CP for instance, had dilapidated and laboured speech and frequent abrupt stops where rapid articulatory action was required. Further, it was used to exemplify why their articulation was not coordinated with breathing and vocalizations and the need for exercises to strengthen the breathing musculature to produce speech. However, there was need for a more specific theory to describe the type of sentences produced by children with DS and CP. In that case, the Systemic Theory was adopted to cover the shortcomings of the Motor Theory in relation to syntactic structures.

2.3.4   Systemic Theory.

Systemic Theory is a theory of meaning as choice by which, language or any other semiotic system is interpreted as networks of interlocking options. Applied to the description of language, it means starting with the most general features (Theme) and proceeding step by step, to even become more specific (Rheme). A message is either about doing or about thinking or about being.

According to Halliday (1985), the structure which gives the clause its character as a message is known as thematic structure. In English, the clause is organized as a message by having a special status assigned to one part of it. One element in the clause is enunciated as the Theme; this then combines with the remainder so that the two parts

28

together constitute a message. The Theme is the element which serves as the point of departure of the message; it is that with which the clause is concerned. The remainder of the message, the part in which the theme is developed, is called in Prague school terminology, the Rheme. As a message structure therefore, a clause consists of Theme accompanied by Rheme. Whatever is chosen as the theme is put first.

This study focused on the tenet of clause as message in the analysis of the syntactic structures produced by children with DS and CP. The study sought to establish whether the sentences these children produced had a Theme and Rheme as posited by Halliday (1985).

Summary of the chapter

Having looked at the literature review and the theoretical framework, the study now shifts its focus to the research methodology that guided the collection of data, with special focus on sampling techniques, data collection and analysis methods.

29

CHAPTER THREE

3.0   RESEARCH METHODOLOGY

3.1   Research Design

A research design is a specific plan for studying the research problem (Mutai, 2000). In order to achieve the objectives of this study, a descriptive case study design was used to explore and describe the characteristics of the population.

This design was considered appropriate for this study since through it, it was possible to administer interview schedules to a sample of teachers in Maria Magdalena Special School for the Mentally Handicapped. It was also possible to observe the sampled children with DS and CP, record their linguistic data, analyse and interpret it before drawing an informed conclusion.

3.2   Site of study

This study was conducted in Central Province, Thika District. The school chosen through purposive sampling was Maria Magdalena Special School for the Mentally Handicapped, situated in Munyu sub-location of Gatuanyaga, approximately twenty four kilometers from Thika town. The School has a student population of ninety, thirteen teachers and a total of seven classes. The school was chosen due to the fact that most of the children here with DS and CP have mild to moderate conditions and therefore, are suitable for the purpose of our study.

3.3   Target population

Basically, the target population of this study encompassed all mentally challenged and neurologically impaired learners in Kenya, whose conditions are mild to moderate, thereby, making them educable. However, considering the time span of the study, this would be too large and demanding a group to deal with. Since the study was about speech development in children with DS and CP at Maria Magdalena Special School for the Mentally Handicapped, the target population included six of these children in the Nursery class, four in Pre-Primary, four in Primary one, two in primary two and four in Primary three classes at the school. The numbers were arrived at after carrying out a survey of the student population of children with DS and CP conditions in the school. A total of 20 children purposively sampled were observed. Specifically, those with DS and CP were used in the study. Five teachers in charge of the five classes sampled were also interviewed.

3.4 Sampling Techniques

Purposive sampling was used to sample Maria Magdalena Special School as the site for the study. This was due to the fact that most children with DS and CP in the school have mild to moderate conditions of mental and neurological handicap therefore, suitable for this study. The study was designed to assess speech development in children with DS and CP and the techniques used by teachers in this school to enhance development of speech among such children. This therefore demanded for the purposive sampling of the special school and the children within the school that filled the criteria of speech deficit. The selection of these children was done in a cross-sectional manner in order to indicate the lack of speech among those sampled and its subsequent development after the intervention techniques were employed over a period of time.

The categories of children with DS and CP found in this school and sampled purposively enabled the researcher collect relevant data for this study, in relation to speech delay and the techniques used by teachers to facilitate speech development in these children. The two groups were chosen since studies showed that DS was the most common and perhaps best known genetic disorder associated with mental challenge and developmental disabilities among them, delayed onset of speech (Beirne-Smith et al,

2006). On the other hand, CP is a motor or movement disorder that resulted in muscle weakness, poor muscle control and coordination, and difficulties in developing speech (Peacock, 2000). The two categories thus, answered the research questions and met the objectives of the study.

3.5 Sample size

Maria Magdalena Special School has a class system comprising of Nursery, Pre-primary, Primary one, Primary two, Primary three, Pre-vocational and Vocational class. The Nursery up to Primary three class has a population of ten, six, seven, six and nine students respectively. The students are not evenly distributed according to gender. The study only focused on children with DS and CP in the Nursery up to Primary three classes, since they fall within the age bracket of 8 – 16 years that the study was interested in. The nursery sample was chosen to reflect the point of entry for most children when without or with minimal speech and, as they first got exposed to the speech techniques. Due to the limiting number of children with DS and CP in the sampled classes and as established during the pilot study, an unequal number of boys and girls with defining characteristics were accessed in the study.

The study adopted a sample of six children with DS and CP, without or with minimal speech in the Nursery class, four without or with minimal speech in Pre-Primary, four with minimal or adequate speech in primary one, two with minimal or adequate speech in Primary two and four with minimal or adequate speech in primary three classes. This covered a total of twenty children at the beginners, intermediate and terminal levels, which also reflected the phases of intervention techniques. The study therefore, observed cumulative groups with DS and CP and who had been exposed to speech techniques. Children with DS and CP were sampled because studies have established that they have delayed onset of speech, which was the focus of this study. Five teachers in charge of the classes were interviewed and their responses recorded on tape and paper. Code names, 'DS' for Down's syndrome and 'CP' for Cerebral palsy were used to refer to both the respondents and the condition suffered. This was in order to protect their identity and for ethical reasons.

3.6 Data Collection Procedures

After obtaining the research permit from relevant authorities, the researcher visited the institution to be used in the study and embarked on data collection. The interview schedule (Ref: App. A1; p.109) used was semi-structured, using both open-ended and closed-ended items, in order to elicit as much information as possible to help answer the research questions. The interview based on an interview schedule between the teachers and the researcher was recorded on tape and later transcribed, before the data was finally analysed and interpreted.

The linguistic output of children with DS and CP sampled was observed and recorded using an observation checklist (Ref: App. A1; p.111). Each activity lasted twenty minutes due to the low concentration span in these children. A total of twenty five observations were made; five per sampled class.

3.7 Research Instruments

Qualitative data was obtained from semi-structured interviews, tape-recording and observation.

a) Interview

The type of mental or neurological handicap of the sampled children, their CA, speech ability and their current class were established using face-to-face interviews between the researcher and the teachers in charge of the sampled classes.   The various speech intervention techniques employed by these teachers were also established and discussed using structured interview schedule (Ref: App. A1; p.109).

b) Tape recording

Tape recording was used as a backup for the interview and during observation. This helped capture accurately the spoken language of children with DS and CP and whatever techniques that were emerging between the teachers and these children during class interactions. This was meant to assist the study to preserve important information that could be made reference to later for systematic analysis.

c) Observation

Participant observation was used to collect sounds, words and sentences produced by these children. This information was recorded using an observation checklist (Ref: App. A1; p.111). Participation gave the researcher an intuitive understanding of what was happening in natural setting among children with DS and CP (Kombo and Tromp, 2006).

3.8 Data analysis procedures.

After data collection, the researcher coded and analysed all data obtained from interview schedules, observation schedules, tape recording and documentary method. The tape recorded data was transcribed, translated, typed and stored on a flash disk. Since the interview guides were structured questions, the qualitative data analysis procedure was employed.

The data about each child was discussed, analyzed and presented in the following order: child's background information which included the child's CA, speech ability before and now, type of mental challenge, the current class and the number of years the child had stayed in the school.

The validity of the study data was assessed in respect to the proposed questions, objectives and assumptions. The synthesized data and findings were presented qualitatively through descriptions and quantitatively using inferential statistics. The speech ability of children with DS and CP, realised spontaneously and observed during the study was presented using sounds, words and sentences. Their speech ability in relation to clause as message was discussed analysed and presented using percentage frequency table.

To test the relationship between the CA of these children and speech development, percentage frequencies were calculated based on the number of complete and defective structures in each age bracket vis-à-vis age. The frequencies were calculated using the formula:

$$\%\text{freq} = \frac{\text{freq} \times 100}{\text{Total}}$$

The resulting information was presented using frequency graphs. Techniques used and their role in the development of speech were discussed and analysed in relation to how frequently each was put into use and the resulting speech ability of children with DS and CP at the time of this study. The findings were presented using descriptive analysis of the data collected.

The validity of the study data was interpreted in relation to the Literature in the theories that guided this study. The researcher sought to establish whether what theories say about development of speech in children with DS and CP was reflected in the data collected.

3.9 Data management and Ethical considerations.

Before embarking on data collection, permission was sought from the Department of English and Linguistics, Kenyatta University. The researcher also sought permission from the authorities in Maria Magdalena Special School to access and interact with the sampled children. The teacher respondents in the research were requested to do so voluntarily.

The purpose of the research was explained to the sampled individuals. Protecting the rights and welfare of the participants should be the major ethical obligation of all parties involved in a research study (Mugenda, 2008). In line with this, the information gathered in the course of this research work will remain confidential, except for the purposes of this study.

Summary of the chapter

This chapter presented the research methodology used in the collection and analysis of data. The next chapter deals with the study data, its presentation and subsequent analysis.

CHAPTER FOUR

DATA ANALYSIS AND PRESENTATION

4.0 INTRODUCTION

The preceding chapter focused on the methodology employed in collecting and handling the study data. This chapter deals with the presentation and analysis of this data on speech development in children with DS and CP. It looks at the nature of the speech ability of the respondents as reflected in their spoken data and the relationship that exists between their CA and speech development. Further, the speech techniques used to promote speech in children with DS and CP are also discussed.

4.1 Speech ability at the time of this study

This study sought to establish the speech ability of children with DS and CP in Maria Magdalena special school in Thika. To achieve this, it observed 20 purposively sampled pupils in the school. It was particularly interested in what is peculiar in their speech, as compared to the speech of normally developing children, with special focus on complete structures and defective ones with omission, substitution and insertion. To achieve this, the study relied on observation of classroom proceedings during which the teacher posed spontaneous questions to which the pupils gave spontaneous responses. It was from these responses and out of class interactions among these children that the study assessed their speech ability. Oral interviews with the teachers were also used where the need to make sense of incomprehensible utterances, seek clarification or further informed explanations arising from findings of this study arose.

This study first drew attention to the ability to make complete structures among the respondents in the progressive levels of Nursery, Pre-Primary, Primary one, Primary two and Primary three. To achieve this, this study took into account the direct questions the teachers posed to the pupils at the various class levels and the responses the questions elicited. The study also sought to establish whether apart from the commonly used declarative clauses, the use of imperative and interrogative clauses emerged in the pupils' utterances and whether these were individual effort or a product of prompting.

4.1.1 Complete clauses

The complete structures addressed by this study are sentences that are complete structurally, phrases as observed in imperatives and single words that however, do communicate adequately within given contexts. Complete structures manifested themselves in declarative, interrogative and imperative clauses.

4.1.1.1 Declarative clauses

In the Nursery class, the teacher posed spontaneous questions to specific pupils, using both Kiswahili and English and got the following responses:

1. Question   **Answer**

i) Mama anafanya nini?   CP1-9: Anapika

What is mother doing?   *She is cooking*

ii).Mnafanya nini?   CP1-9: Tunakula

What are you doing?   *We are eating*

iii). Uliletwa na nani shuleni?   CP3-11: Baba

Who brought you to school?   *Father*

Example (i) and (ii) are complete clauses in Kiswahili with clause elements such as subject *[A]* and *[Tu]*, present tense marker *[na]* and verbs *[pika]* and *[kula]* respectively. In example (iii), the noun *'baba'* **(father)** was used to respond to the teacher's question, instead of a complete sentence *'Nililetwa shuleni na baba yangu'* **(I was brought to**

school by my father). However, the one word response is considered a complete sentence because it does communicate effectively within context. In the pre-primary class, the following three spontaneous questions were posed by the teacher and spontaneous responses realized from the individual pupils addressed;

2. Question	**Answer**
i) What is this?	CP4-12: Table
ii) Shule yenu inaitwaje?	CP4: Shule yetu inaitwa Maria
	Magdalena
What is the name of your school?	*Our school is called Maria*
	Magdalena

A single word response **(table)** has been used in example (i) to respond to the teacher's question. However, a complete simple clause entailing clause elements such as a noun phrase, *'shule yetu'* **(our school),** a verb phrase, *'inaitwa'* **(is called)** and a complement **(Maria Magdalena)** are used in the response in example (ii) above. The teacher in primary one class also posed questions to the pupils and the responses realized are presented below:

3. Question	**Answer**
i)Hii ni nini?	DS7-12: Dirisha
What is this?	*Window*
ii) Hiki ni nini?	CP6-13: Kiti
What is this?	*Chair*
iii) Mama yako yuko wapi?	CP7-13: Mama yangu yuko nyumbani
Where is your mother?	*My mother is at home*

This study noted that single word responses, *'dirisha'* **(window)** and *'kiti'* **(chair)** were used in example (i) and (ii) above by DS7 aged twelve and CP6 aged thirteen respectively. This occurred after their teacher asked them to identify items in their classes. On the other hand, a complete simple Kiswahili clause *'Mama yangu yuko nyumbani'* **(My mother is at home)** was used in example (iii) by respondent CP7 aged thirteen. The clause has the following clause elements: a subject- *'mama yangu'* **(my mother)**, a subject marker and a verb- *'yuko'* **(is)** and a prepositional phrase- *'nyumbani'* **(at home).** In primary two class, three questions were posed to the pupils spontaneously by the teacher. The questions and answers were:

4. Question_   **Answer**

i) Hii ni nini?   DS8-16: Makasi

What is this?   *A pair of scissors*

iii) Nitapikiwa nini kwenu?   CP8-16: Watakupikia mayai na chapati.

What will they cook for me in your place?   *They will cook for you eggs and chapati.*

A single word is used in example (i) in response to a question posed by the teacher. On the other hand, a complete declarative clause is used by CP8 aged sixteen, in example (iii) to respond to the teacher's question. The clause, *'Watakupikia mayai na chapati'* **(They will cook for you eggs and *chapati*)** has a subject 'wa' **(they),** future tense marker *'ta'* **(will),** an object marker *'ku'* **(you)**, an applied verb *'pikia'* **(cook for)** and a compound noun phrase entailing coordination *'mayai na chapati'* **(eggs and *chapati*).** The teacher in primary three also posed questions and the spontaneous responses given by pupils are presented below:

5. Question   **Answer**

(i) What is your name?   CP9-16: My name is Francis Kimani.

(ii) Utaambia mgeni nini?   DS10-16: Tumeshukuru

What will you tell the visitor?   *We are grateful*

Example (i) is a complete sentence with the following clause elements: a subject **(my name),** verb **(is)** and a complement **(Francis Kimani).** Example (ii) is also a complete clause consisting of a subject *'Tu'* **(we),** tense marker *'me'* **(are)** and a verb *'shukuru'* **(thank).**

From the findings presented above, this study established that despite the challenges experienced by children with DS and CP, they are still able to make complete structures in their speech. This occurs during communication whether amongst themselves or with any other party with normal brain functioning, which in this case included the teachers and the researcher. The examples accruing from fieldwork that this study has discussed in the preceding sections indicate the use of either complete simple clauses entailing clause elements such as subject, verb and complement *(My name is Francis Kimani),* a compound noun phrase entailing coordination *(chai na mkate)* or single words *(makasi).*

As far as single word responses are concerned, it emerged that 15 out of the 20 respondents sampled had difficulties handling longer grammatical units and simply gave one word responses even upon prompting. This accounted for 75% of the respondents, which this study finds an authoritative basis to conclude that children with DS and CP find handling long grammatical units a challenge and therefore prefer short or single word sentences. The teachers submit that from their experience and research, the paralysis of speech muscles, especially among

children with CP and their inability to control breath in order to produce speech, affects the production of long grammatical units (Kaburu and Wanjiru, 2009: Personal interview). They derive much of their argument based on the Motor Theory by Ladefoged (1982), which states that all speech is the product of motor behaviour and muscular movement of the vocal organs. This study therefore submits that based on the professional views of the teachers and the library resource cited, reflexes and centrally generated motor commands of the children accessed by this study lack coordination due to undeveloped motor system in the speech centre in the brain. This explains their conditional tendency to use words or shorter sentences. Nevertheless, this study notes that despite the tendency to use ellipses in responses by children with DS and CP, the single words still communicate semantically.

4.1.1.2 Imperative Clauses

Besides words, phrases and longer grammatical units of the declarative type, other complete structures in this study data included imperative clauses which are presented in the section below:

6.Imperative	Gloss
i).Nyamaza (command)	CP6-13: Keep quiet
ii).Amka (command)	CP6-13: Wake up
iii).Nyamazeni tuombe (request)	CP1-9: Keep quiet we pray
iv).Nipe (command)	CP2-9: Give me

In example (i), (ii) and (iv) above, imperatives signaling a command were used by the respondents. The commands were directed at their classmates. On the other hand, the imperative used by CP1 (*Nyamazeni tuombe*) is a polite request. As observed during this study, the respondent politely requested her classmates to maintain silence so that she can make a prayer, a request that was granted with the help of the teacher.

This study noted that imperatives occurred in a discourse involving the pupils only. However, the teachers pointed out that they also occur when the pupils feel tired and irritable or as they fight over toys in class as was observed with CP2 aged nine. He ordered his classmate to give him back a toy by saying '*Nipe*' **(give me).** The study also observed that although the imperatives lack complete clause structure such as SVO, they stand complete and communicative within the contexts in which they occur. For example, the phrase '*Amka*' **(wake up)** is a command uttered by CP6 and directed at a classmate who had fallen asleep at her desk. However, what the respondent should have said is: '*Ninataka uamke*' **(I want you to wake up)** if the structure was a declarative one. The phrase consists of only a verb '*mka*' **(wake)** and a preposition '*A*' **(up)** instead of a subject '*Ni*' **(I)**, present tense marker '*na*', a verb '*taka*' **(want)**, an object marker '*U*' **(you)** and an infinitive '*amke*' **(to wake up).** Going by the structure of imperative clauses, the clause above is considered complete. It still communicates its meaning effectively within context despite the ellipsis.

The study also established that complete structures observed in the speech of the respondents included interrogative clauses as illustrated below:

7. Interrogatives	Gloss
i).Unatoka wapi?	DS7-12: You come from where?
ii).Unaitwa nani?	CP9-16: Your name is who?
iii).Kwenu ni wapi?	CP4-12: Your home is where?
iv).Tutafunga siku gani	CP8-16: We close school when?

The questions in example (i), (ii) and (iii) were posed by pupils to the researcher. On the other hand, example (iv) was a question directed to the teacher in primary two by respondent CP8 aged sixteen respectively. When analysed, the imperative clause, '*Kwenu ni wapi?* **(Your home is where?)** can be said to consist of a subject '*kwenu*' **(your home),** a verb 'ni' **(is)** and a WH-Interrogative '*wapi*' **(where).** Note that unlike in English where the WH-Interrogative is fronted, in Kiswahili it is placed at the end of the interrogating sentence. This study observed that only the WH-questions were used as opposed to YES-NO questions. This can

be explained by the fact that the interrogative clauses realised during this study were not produced voluntarily but in imitation of the teachers. The teachers inferred that the existing low levels of intelligence among children with MH for instance, interferes with their ability to construct a variety of clauses on their own. Three of the questions above were posed by children with CP. This confirms what studies say about such children. Ianneli (2005) notes that although the

average intelligence is considered to be around an IQ of 100. The measured intelligence of individuals with mental handicap is somewhere around 70 or below, depending on the severity.

Cumulatively, this study established that the number of respondents who used imperative and interrogative sentences was lower than that of respondents who used declarative sentences. Out o the 20 respondents (n=20) observed by this study, 6=30% only used interrogative sentences, 4=20% used imperative sentences while 10=50% showed inclination towards declarative sentences. Since in normal daily speech people do communicate largely using declarative sentences, this finding showed that children with DS and CP exhibit the same sentence types.

This study observed that no respondent used exclamative sentences although there were situations that called for their use. For example, respondent CP3 simply uses the adjective 'smart' **(mart)** whose initial sound is omitted, to describe her teacher's hair. In normal circumstances, the respondent should have invoked the exclamative, **'How smart your hair is',** in order to make her strong feelings known. The teachers pointed out that children with DS especially, are incapable of expressing strong feelings except for those of anger, annoyance and irritation expressed through imperative sentences. This affirms what Ianneli (2005) states that children with mental retardation are somewhat more likely than other children to have behavioural problems such as explosive outbursts, temper tantrums and physical aggressive behaviour.

4.1.2 Defective Structures

The study also set out to establish defective structures present in the speech of the respondents. This was done with special focus on phonological processes such as omission, substitution and insertion of speech sounds and syllables. These processes have been discussed in the preceding chapter (Ref. Ch. 2, sec. 2.2.6.2).

4.1.2.1 Omission of sounds and syllables

By observing classroom proceedings, the study recorded spontaneous responses by pupils to questions posed by their teachers at the various levels, from nursery to primary three. It was observed that children with DS and CP in this study presented speech characterized by omission of sounds as illustrated below:

8. Question   **Answer**

i). Hii ni nini? (*Pointing at a window*)   DS1-12: 'Disa' for 'Dirisha'

What is this?   *Window*

ii).Hii ni nini? (*Touching pupil's neck*)   CP10-16: 'ingo' for 'Shingo'

                                                   Neck

iii).What colour is this *(pointing at colour red)*   DS4-10: 'ed' for 'Red'

iv).What colour is this? *(Pointing at colour green)*   CP5-13: 'Geen' for 'Green'

v).What is this? *(Pointing at a book)*   CP10-16: 'ooku' for 'Book'

In example (i), the voiceless palato-alveolar fricative /   / in word medial position has been omitted in the word *'dirisha'* **(window)**. The same sound is omitted in the word *'shingo'* (neck) in example (v) by respondent CP10. This sound is articulated in close approximation. The passage of the air between the two articulators is so narrow that as the air passes between them, there is friction accompanying the sound produced. In example (iii), the alveolar trill / r / in word initial position is omitted by respondent DS4 in the adjective 'Red'. Similarly, in example (iv), respondent CP5 pronounces the word *'green'* as *'geen'* when asked by the teacher to name one of the colours in class, consequently, omitting the same alveolar trill in word medial position. The trill is articulated with a complete closure and open approximation. The tip of the tongue touches the alveolar ridge completely and is trilled against it. The omission may be explained by the fact that in the word 'green', the place and manner of articulation for the voiced velar stop, / g / and the trill are different.

Although both sounds are articulated with a complete closure, the trill differs in that it is produced with open approximation and tip of the tongue trilling. The production of the two consonants therefore requires quick coordinated movements from one motor programme to another, from one point of articulation (alveolar) to another (velar). The omission could be explained by the fact that the mechanism involved in the trilling and the shift in place and manner of articulation is elusive to the respondents. The teachers attribute this to mental handicap and paralysis affecting the production of speech sounds in words. This reinforces what Shriver (2010) states that expressive skills in children with DS and CP may be severely disordered largely because of mental handicap and neuromuscular impairment. This affects the functioning of the articulators as well as other speech organs.

This study observed that the respondents also omitted syllables in words. Below is an illustration:

9. Question   **Answer**

i). Hii ni nini? (Pointing at a window)   CP6-13: 'Disa' for 'Dirisha

What is this?   *Window*

ii). Mlikunywa chai saa ngapi?	DS1-12: Pema' for 'mapema'
When did you take tea?	*Early*
iii). Unaishi na nani?	CP2-9: 'Ba" for 'Baba'
Whom do you live with?	*Father*
iv). Hii ni nini? (Pointing at a basin)	CP3-11: "Kai for 'Karai'
What is this?	*Basin*
v).Hii ni nini (pointing at a bottle of oil)	CP3-11: 'ta' for 'Mafuta'
What is this?	*Oil*
vi). Huyu ni nani? (Pointing at Researcher)	CP10-16: 'Mu' for 'Mwalimu'
Who is this?	DS8-16 *Teacher*

In example (i), the word *'Dirisha'* (**window**) had its medial syllable *[ri]* omitted by respondent DS1 and CP6 respectively. This occurred after they were asked by their respective teachers to name the window in class. Similarly, the word *'Mapema'* (**early**) in example (ii) has its initial syllable *[ma]* omitted. This occurs in the speech of DS1 aged twelve. In example (iii), respondent CP2 aged nine omits a syllable *[ba]* in word final position of the noun *'baba'* (**father**). An initial *[ma]* and medial syllable *[fu]* are omitted from the word *'mafuta'* (oil) in example (v), by respondent CP3 and CP10 aged eleven and sixteen respectively. The omission occurred when they were asked by their teachers to identify a bottle of body oil in their classes.

Similarly, respondent DS8 and CP10, both aged sixteen, omit three syllables in the word *'Mwalimu'* (**teacher**) when asked to identify a teacher and the researcher respectively. In word initial position, the syllabic consonant *[m]* is omitted while in word medial position, two syllables *[wa]* and *[li]* are omitted. The Kiswahili syllable structure and the status of nasal sounds as syllabic consonants have been discussed in detail under the Literature review (Ref. Ch. 2, sec.2.2.6.2). It can be argued that the omissions occur because producing a syllabic consonant needs a lot of effort. Where a syllabic nasal occurs, most speakers will introduce a vowel for easy articulation (Ngugi & Macharia, 2006).

Going by the study data pertaining to omission and part of which is presented above, a summary can be made that only 6 out of the 16 structures recorded had omission of sounds. The rest involved omission of syllables. In addition, the study noted that the highest number of omissions was in word initial and medial positions as opposed to word final position. This study therefore concluded that omission of syllables is more prevalent than that of sounds and that, word initial position is the most recurrent. This could imply that the take off is tricky. The affected children fail to gather enough air in the lungs to be able to pronounce whole words. The teachers pointed out that children with DS and CP have difficulties initiating speech and consequently, articulate final syllables only.

This study therefore agrees with what Dockrell & Messer (1999) state that all speech sounds are made with some movement of air and that the aggressive pulmonic is by far the most commonly used. However, the child with mental handicap and neurological impairment may be able to inhale deeply but unable to control exhalation which is the most needed for speech. It can thus be argued that children with DS and CP are unable to carry out coordinative movements of the respiratory, laryngeal and oral muscles for articulation due to poor control of exhalation, resulting in the omissions.

4.1.2.2 Substitution of Sounds

Ingram (1976) defines substitution as a case where a sound is replaced by another without reference to neighbouring sounds. This study sought to examine the speech ability of children with DS and CP with reference to how often they substituted sounds in words. To achieve this, the study relied on observation of classroom and out- of-classroom interactions. The study recorded spontaneous responses by pupils arising from spontaneous questions raised by teachers. In the nursery class for instance, the teacher posed questions and the following responses were realised from two out of the six children accessed in this study:

13. Question	Answer
i).Hii ni nini *(teacher pointing at her teeth)*	DS1-12:'Ng'eno' for 'Meno'
What is this?	*Teeth*
(ii).Sema 'namba'	DS1: 'Mamba' for 'namba'
Say 'Number	*Number*
iii). Mlikula nini leo	CP3-11: 'mama' for 'nyama'
What did you eat today?	*Meat*

The data above depicted the substitution of sounds in words by respondent DS1 and CP3 respectively. In example (i), the bilabial nasal / m / occurring in word initial position is substituted with the velar nasal / / sound in the word *'meno'* **(teeth).** In example (ii), the bilabial nasal /m/ is used to substitute the alveolar nasal /n/ occurring in word initial position in the word *'namba'* **(Number).** In example (iii), the palatal nasal / / occurring in word initial position is substituted with the bilabial nasal / m / in the word *'Nyama'* **(meat).** The substitutions may be caused by the inaccessibility of motor programmes responsible for the production of alveolar and palatal sounds. Ladefoged (1982) states that motor deficiencies of the tongue and other speech organs make it difficult for these children to produce speech. This is because all speech is the product of motor behaviour and muscular movement of the vocal organs.

The teacher in the pre-primary class also posed random questions to her class and the following spontaneous responses were given by the pupils:

14. Question	**Answer**
i).Hii ni nini?(*Showing pupil a drawing*)	DS5-11:'Mombe' for 'Ng'ombe'
What is this?	*Cow*
ii).What do we call this? (*Pointing at the table*)	CP5-13: 'Kable for 'table'
iii).What is this? *(Pointing at a chair)*	CP5: 'Kair' for 'Chair'
iv).What is this? *(Teacher touching her head)*	CP5: 'Heag' for 'Head'

In the first example, respondent DS5 aged eleven substitutes the velar nasal/ / in word initial position with the bilabial nasal /m/ in the word *'Ng'ombe'* **(Cow)**. Both sounds are articulated with a complete closure although the point of closure for the bilabial nasal is at the lips while that for the velar nasal is at the hard palate. Similarly, respondent CP5 aged thirteen makes numerous substitutions in her speech as exemplified above. In example (ii), the voiceless alveolar plosive / t / occurring in word initial position is substituted with voiceless velar plosive /k/ in the word *'Table'*. Both sounds are oral stops and are articulated with a complete closure. However, the point of closure for the alveolar plosive is at the hard palate while that of the velar plosive is at the soft palate. The word *'Chair''* in example (iii) has its initial voiceless alveolar affricate / / substituted with the voiceless velar plosive /k/. The alveolar affricate is articulated with open approximation while the velar plosive is articulated with a complete closure. In example (iv), the alveolar plosive / d / occurring in word final position is substituted with the voiced velar plosive / g / in the word *'Head'*. Both sounds are articulated with a complete closure. However, the point of closure for the alveolar plosive is at the soft palate while that of the velar plosive is at the velum. The difference in place of articulation may be the reason for the substitution. Zattore and Gandour (2008) state that in order for sounds to be produced correctly, the lips, tongue, jaw, velum

and larynx must make accurate movements at the right time otherwise, the intended sounds become distorted.

The study observed that respondent CP5 constantly substituted all the alveolar and palatal sounds with velar sounds, whether occurring in word initial, medial or final positions. Her class teacher pointed out that the child suffered frequent throat infection, details of which appear in the background information (Ref: App. A2, p.112). Her teacher pointed out that the paralysis affecting her speech muscles made her speech incomprehensible. This confirms Peacock's (2000) view that people with CP have difficulty with muscle control and coordination, since the motor control areas of their brain are affected by the condition suffered.

In primary three class, the teacher also posed spontaneous questions to respondent CP10 aged sixteen who gave the following responses that had sounds in them substituted:

15. Question   **Answer**

i).Mtakula nini leo?   CP10-16: 'Mama' for 'nyama'

   What will you eat today?   *Meat*

ii).Hii ni nini? (*Pointing at a tape recorder*)   CP10: 'yedio' for 'redio'

   What is this?   *Radio*

iii).Nikuletee nini kesho   CP10: 'twiti for 'switi

   What do I bring you tomorrow?   *Sweet*

All the examples of substitution presented above occurred in the speech of CP10 aged sixteen. In example (i), the palatal nasal /   / occurring in word initial position is substituted with the bilabial nasal / m / in the word *'nyama'* (**meat**). In example (ii), the alveolar trill / r / occurring in word initial position is substituted with the palatal approximant / j / in the word *'Radio'* which is pronounced as *'yedio'*. The word *'Switi'* (**sweet**) in example (iii) is pronounced as *'twiti'*. The voiceless alveolar fricative / s / articulated in close approximation is substituted with the voiceless alveolar plosive / t /

which is articulated with a complete closure. The substitution occurs in word initial position. The teachers indicated that the respondent has difficulties moving muscles associated with speech production in order to produce speech. This affirms Finnie's (2004) assertion that some children with CP have a lot of difficulty moving the muscles that control the sound making operation. The length of vocalizations is generally short, due to lack of breath support. Damage to the neuromuscular site involved in the execution of speech movements may affect strength and timing of muscle contraction (Dancie, 2009).

It was noted that both primary one and primary two classes had no structures with substitution in them. However, there were two cases of omissions noted in these classes and discussed earlier in this section (Ref. sec. 4.1.2.1, p.58).

This study concluded that the respondents appeared to substitute sounds they found to be problematic with those they could easily articulate. This substitution occurred in all word positions. However, it was observed that substitution in word initial position was more prevalent than medial and final. For instance, out of the 12 examples discussed above, 11 had substitution in word initial position and one, in word final position. It can be argued that substitution is caused by the inaccessibility of the motor programmes responsible for the production of the sounds substituted, especially when they occur in word initial position. This affirms what Ladefoged (1982) proposed that in the speech motor planning stage, motor goals are specified to formulate action strategies for example, close lips and raise soft palate for / b / in the word 'boy'. Then these actions are translated into speech motor programmes that specify what particular muscles will act, with what force and what time to achieve the speech target, in view of the contextual conditions. It can be said that the motor goals of the children used in this study fail to formulate action strategies to produce the sounds substituted.

4.1.2.3: Insertion

This study also sought to establish the speech ability of children with DS and CP by assessing the number of times the respondents inserted sounds in words. This was achieved by observing proceedings inside and out of the classroom. The study recorded the following questions from the teachers and spontaneous responses from the pupils. The teacher in the pre-primary class posed spontaneous questions and respondent DS4 gave the response below; the only one with insertion in it:

16. Question_   **Answer**

(i)Hii ni rangi gani? (Pointing at the colour black)   DS4-10:'Bulack'for 'black'

What colour is this?

In the example above, respondent DS4 aged ten pronounces the word 'black' as *'bulack'* in response to the teacher's question. A high back vowel / u / is inserted in word medial position. Similarly, the teacher in primary three class posed questions and a spontaneous response with a case of insertion was given by respondent CP10:

17. Question   **Answer**

i).What is this (*showing pupil a book*)   CP10-16: 'ooku' for 'book'

In pronouncing the word *'book'*, a high back vowel / u / is inserted in word final position. Note that the omission in the same word was discussed in the preceding section (Ref. section 4.1.2.1, p.58). It can be argued that the process of insertion is used to ease the pronunciation of the words in question, by adopting the more comfortable CV Kiswahili syllable structure. This can be explained by what studies say that in acquiring language, the CV structure precedes the CC structure. According to Bowen (1998), the consonant cluster demands for the manipulation of different articulating organs, something that is elusive to even normal speakers. Vowels are occasionally inserted to break consonant clusters.

The study observed that cases of insertion did not arise in the nursery, primary one and primary two classes. However, they were also rare in the classes they were observed in as exemplified above. This could be attributed to speech advancement in these children as a result of maturity, speech techniques used and exposure to an educative environment. This affirms what Shriver (2010) says that mental handicap, as observed in children with DS in this study, is not a static phenomenon, but can be dependant on upbringing and education.

Going by the study data presented on defective speech in children with DS and CP, it can be concluded that the phonological processes of omission, substitution and insertion affect both groups of children, irrespective of the chronological age attained. For instance, respondent DS5 aged eleven and respondent CP10 both aged sixteen displayed defective speech. However, going by the total number of the respondents who produced defective speech, the study concluded that the process of omission with a frequency of 9, was more prevalent compared to that of substitution (5) and insertion (2). This observation reinforces what Algozzine et al (2006) state that children with DS and CP display delayed and defective speech, due to the condition involved. Such children struggle tremendously to complete the same tasks that many of their peers do without difficulty.

4.1.3: Thematic Analysis of the speech of children with DS and CP
The study also sought to establish whether children with CP and DS displayed both Theme and Rheme in their speech structures. This study aimed at observing the usage of Theme (the element which serves as the point of departure of the message) and Rheme (the remaining part on which the theme is developed). To this end, the Systemic Theory

by Halliday (1985) guided both the collection of data and its subsequent analysis. The details of this theory were discussed in Chapter two (Ref: sec. 2.3.4, p.37). The analysis of the clause has been done using Halliday's thematic structure analysis. This is illustrated below:

18. Question   **Answer**

(i)What is your name?   CP9-16: My name is Francis Kimani.

(ii)Mama yako yuko wapi?   CP7-13: Mama yangu yuko nyumbani

Where is your mother?   *My mother is at home.*

(iii)Mama yako anafanya nini?   CP7: Anapika.

What is your mother doing?   *She is cooking*

(iv)Mnafanya nini   CP1-9: Tunakula.

What are you doing?   *We are eating.*

In the examples given, the clauses contain both Theme and Rheme. Their components as clauses were discussed in section 4.2.1 of this chapter under complete speech (Ref. p. 49). The Thematic analysis is presented in the table below:

Table 4.1: Clauses with Theme and Rheme.

My name	is Francis Kimani.
Mama yangu (*my mother)*	yuko nyumbani *(is at home)*
A *(she)*	napika *(is cooking)*
Tu *(We)*	nakula *(are eating)*
Theme	**Rheme**

The study also focused on interrogative clauses in the collection of data. This was achieved by the teachers prompting the respondents to ask questions. The teachers posed questions and asked the pupils to repeat after them. The thematic analysis of the interrogative clauses using the Systemic Theory is presented below:

19. Question

(i) DS7-12: Unatoka wapi?

   You come from where?

(ii) CP8-16: Tutafunga siku gani?

   We close school when?

(iii) CP9-16: Unaitwa nani?

   You are called who?

(iv) CP4-12: Kwenu ni wapi?

   Your home is where?

Table 4.2: Analysis of WH – Interrogatives.

Unatoka *You come from*	wapi? *where?*
Tutafunga siku *We close school*	gani? *when?*
Unaitwa *You are called*	nani? *who?*
Kwenu ni *Your home is*	wapi? *where?*
Theme	**Rheme**

According to Halliday (1985), the WH-Interrogative is always the Theme since it is the element that requests the information. What comes first is what is considered a Theme. However, the WH-Interrogative comes last in the Kiswahili clauses. It follows the principle of the end focus. It is therefore a case of a marked theme since what would be a Rheme in English functions as a Theme in the Kiswahili clauses. The WH-Interrogative becomes the Rheme. The study also sought to analyse the Theme-Rheme pattern in imperative clauses. The examples are presented below:

20. Question

i) CP6-13: Nyamaza (*commanding a classmate*)

      Keep quiet

ii) CP6: Amka (*command directed at a classmate lying on the desk*).

      Wake up.

iii) DS5-11: At ease (*command directed at classmates*).

iv) CP2-9: Nipe (*demanding for a toy from a classmate*)

Give me.

v) CP1-9: Nyamazeni tuombe *(request addressed to classmates)*

Keep quiet we pray.

The imperative clauses above, whose structure was discussed in this section (Ref. 4.1.1.2, p.54) lack explicit Themes. Structurally therefore, they may be considered to be consisting of Rheme only, the thematic component of command or request being left implicit. However, Halliday (1985) says that the clauses can be analysed in either of two ways because of the strong association of first position with thematic value in the clause. For instance, the full clause in example (i) should be *'Ninataka munyamaze'* (**I want you to keep quiet)** and not merely *'Nyamaza'* **(keep quiet).** What is omitted is understood to be *'I want you/us to'*. The two possible analyses of the imperative clause are presented below:

Table 4.3: Analysis of Imperative Clauses

	Nyamaza *(keep quiet)* Amka *(wake up)* Nipe *(give me)* Nyamazeni tuombe(*keep quiet we pray)*
Theme	**Rheme**

The examples above lack explicit Themes. Structurally therefore, they are considered as consisting of Rheme only, the thematic component of request being left implicit. However, because of the strong association of first position with the thematic value in the clause, this structure has the effect of giving the verb the status of a Theme. Halliday

(1985) says such clauses can thus be analysed in either of two ways as shown above and below, for one of the clauses:

Table 4.4: Analysis of Imperative Clauses

Nyamazeni *(keep quiet)*	Tuombe *(we pray)*
Theme	**Rheme**

As far as thematic analysis of the clause is concerned, the table below shows the speech ability of children with DS and CP based on types of sentences realised during the collection of the study data:

Table 4.5: Speech ability in relation to clause as message

CLAUSE AS MESSAGE	SENTENCE TYPE					
	DECLARATIVES		**INTERROGATIVE**		**IMPERATIVE**	
	FREQ	**%**	**FREQ**	**%**	**FREQ**	**%**
Theme and Rheme	24	8.3	12	92.3	-	-
Rheme Only	205	70.9	1	7.7	6	85.7
Partial Rheme	60	20.8	-	-	1	14.3
TOTAL	**289**	**100**	**13**	**100**	**7**	**100**

The table shows that most of the clauses in the data collected have Rheme only at 70.9% for declaratives, 7.7% for interrogatives and 85.7% for imperative sentences. The proportion of complete clauses containing both Theme and Rheme is at 8.3% for declaratives and 92.3% for interrogatives. No imperative clauses produced had both Rheme and Theme. The percentage of clauses with Partial Rheme stood at 20.8% for declaratives and 14.3% for imperative sentences. No partial Rheme was realised in interrogative clauses.

From the data presented in the table, this study noted that the lowest percentage was in clauses with Partial Rheme while the highest percentage occurred in clauses with Rheme only. The study observed that majority of the respondents spoke in single words as opposed to connected speech, consequently, omitting Theme. This could be due to the inaccessibility of the motor programmes responsible for the production of longer stretches of speech due to the condition suffered. This study considered what Cantwell and Baker (1987) state that children with DS and CP lag behind significantly in the development of speech. Even those who learn how to speak after the introduction of speech intervention techniques do communicate in sounds, *words* and uncoordinated sentences only.

The low percentage in clauses with Theme and Rheme within declaratives (8.3%) could be due to the inability of children with DS and CP to produce such clauses or the fact that they do not know them. Halliday (1985) states that in speaking or writing, we consciously signal that an item has status by putting it first. The inability of these children to articulate the forms could be due to the absence of the motor programmes responsible for the production of connected speech to give rise to Theme and Rheme. As stated by Beirne-Smith et al (2006), children with CP especially, experience difficulty in positioning muscle groups used to speak and sequencing their actions to produce long stretches of speech.

On the other hand, the high percentage in clauses with Theme and Rheme in interrogatives (92.3%) can be explained by the fact that most of the responses were not the children's own effort. This study observed that the use of interrogatives among children with DS and CP was not individual effort but a product of imitation and partly, prompting. Lack of clauses with Theme and Rheme in imperative clauses can be explained by the fact that naturally, their structure allows for ellipsis. They are constructed mainly using verbs and prepositions as illustrated above. The subject is ellipsed. Even in the speech of non-handicapped speakers, the same theme-less structures would be realised.

4.2: The relationship between the CA of these children and speech development

In the preceding section, the speech ability of children with DS and CP at the time of this study was discussed. It emerged from the data that these children have speech and communicate using both complete and defective structures. This study also sought to establish the relationship between the CA of these children and speech development. It particularly endeavored to find out whether these children's speech ability progresses as they advance in age, as is the case in normally developing children. To achieve this, the study adopted two methods of collecting data. Participant observation was used to capture classroom discourse that depicted the mastery of speech in children with DS and CP of different ages. On the other hand, semi-structured oral interviews with the teachers were carried out outside class, with a view to obtaining more information that would otherwise be difficult to get through participant observation only.

The percentage frequencies in the findings were calculated based on the number of complete and incomplete structures produced from the total number of questions asked vis-à-vis age. The ages of the respondents ranging from 9-16 years were divided into three brackets: 9-11 years, 12-14 years and 15-16 years respectively as grouped into different progressive classes. Out of the ten respondents with DS observed ranging from 9-16 years; it emerged that not all of them could make complete structures without including incomplete structures, in the course of their speech. The frequencies of this distribution are presented in the graph below:

Fig 4.1: Graph showing the distribution of complete and incomplete structures in children with DS

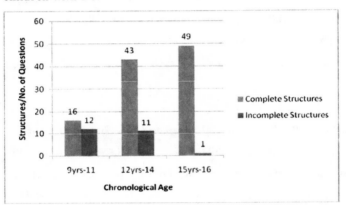

The graph reveals that out of 26 questions asked in the age bracket of 9-11 years, 16 (61.5%) realised complete structures while 10 (46.1%) realised incomplete or

otherwise, defective structures. In the age bracket of 12-14 years, a total of 54 questions were asked out of which 43 (79.6%) gave rise to complete structures while 11 (20.3%) only realised incomplete structures. A total of 50 questions were posed in the age bracket of 15-16 years out of which 49 (98%) responses were complete structures whereas 1 (2%) was an incomplete one. The upper classes had higher stimuli because of their ability to converse freely and respond to questions asked as compared to the lower classes, who suffered constant mood swings.

This study also observed the speech of ten respondents with CP. Of interest was whether the kind of speech produced was in line with the CA of the respondents. The findings are presented in the graph below:

Fig 4.2: Graph showing the distribution of complete and incomplete structures in children with CP

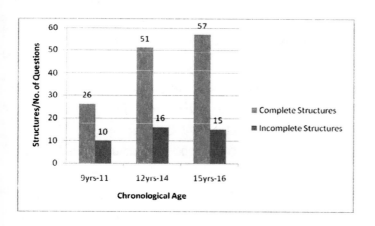

From the graph, we can deduce that 36 questions were asked in the age bracket of 9-11 years, giving rise to 26 (72.2%) complete and 10 (27.8) incomplete structures respectively. In the age bracket of 12-14 years, a total of 67 questions were posed and they realised 51 (76.1%) complete and 16 (23.9% incomplete structures. In the last age bracket of 15-16 years, a total of 72 questions posed gave rise to 57 (79.2%) complete and 15 (20.8%) incomplete structures respectively.

It was therefore observed that overall in all age classes; the percentage of complete structures was higher than that of incomplete structures. The individual percentage of complete structures improves with age. For example, it begins at a low of 61.5% for DS and 72.2% for CP children at age bracket of 9-11 years. This percentage rises to 98% for DS and 79.2% for CP children at the age of 15-16 years. It can therefore be inferred that although these children lag behind in speech, it finally does develop. Advancement in age seems to reflect advancement in speech but at a slower pace than what is observed in normally developing children. This confirms what Inhelder and Woodward (1979) say in the Theory of Cognitive Development. They state that children with DS and CP progress through the same stages of cognitive development as their typically developing peers with the major difference in rate and highest level achieved. As observed in this study, they often have cognitive structures more typical of chronologically younger children.

On the other hand, the percentage of incomplete structures is the reverse. For instance, the production of incomplete structures starts at a high of 46.1% for children with DS and 27.8% for children with CP at the age bracket of 9-11 years respectively. However, this percentage drops to 2% for children with DS and 20.8% for children with CP at the age bracket of 15-16 years. According to the teachers, the growth observed in the data presented above may be due to a number of factors among them, maturity in terms of CA and the communication needs that emerge (Kaburu, 2009: Personal Interview). This seems to reinforce what Piaget (1969) states that the child's ability to think and learn changes with age as the child matures. This study observed that older children in the terminal classes displayed a mastery of complete speech as opposed to incomplete.

This study also noted that children with CP had lower percentages of complete structures compared to children with DS, despite the fact that the latter are known to have a higher prevalence of mental retardation. This may be due to the deficit in motor coordination and timing which adversely affects the speech production system among children with CP. Dancie (2009) affirms that in children with CP, damage to the neuromuscular sites involved in the execution of speech movements may affect strength and timing of muscle contraction.

4.3 Intervention techniques used in speech development

To establish the techniques used in speech development of children with DS and CP, this study adopted two methods of collecting data. Participant observation was used in active class interactions while oral interviews with the teachers were carried out outside class. From this exercise, the study established that the following methods are used by the teachers on all the pupils regardless of the class level. They include communication on one-to-one, use of real objects, use of pictures and drawings, use of the mirror and exercises that involve blowing at or into something. However, for beginners, the most common technique was the use of real objects while for the middle level, imitation was the most used. Communication on one-to-one was the most common at the terminal level.

4.3.1: Communication on one-to-one

This study observed that teachers trained the children in speech by constantly communicating with them on one- to-one. This technique was observed in all the five classes used in this study. The interactive process was done using mainly Kiswahili and occasionally English. It entailed direct communication between the teacher and the pupil without the use of any mediated communication aid. The teachers posed questions to which the pupils were expected to give verbal answers immediately in order to complete a two way communication cycle. In the Nursery class, the teacher involved the pupils in the following interactive process:

23. Question   **Answer**

i) Mama alikuletea nini?   DS1-12: Soda

What did mother bring you?   *Soda*

ii) Mnafanya nini?   CP1-9: Tunakula

   What are you doing?   *We are eating*

The conversational questions posed by the teacher in this class received the responses of *'Soda"* and *'Tunakula'* **(We are eating)**. In the pre-primary class, the following interactive process was observed:

24. Question   **Answer**

i) Unaenda wapi?   DS4-10: Nje

Where are going to?   *Outside*

ii) Mmekaa wapi?   CP4-12: Darasani

Where are you seated?   *In class*

The teacher engaged the children in a conversation and got the responses above. The word *'Nje'* is used to indicate where the respondent is moving to while the phrase *'darasani'* **(in class)** is used to answer a question on where they are seated. The teacher in Primary one class also engaged some of the pupils in the conversation below:

25. Question   **Answer**

i) Kwenu ni wapi?   DS6-13: Ruai

Where is your home?   *Ruai*

ii) Ulikula nini?   CP7-13: Mchele

What did you eat?   *Rice*

Asked where their home is in example (i), the pupil responds by naming a place- *Ruai*. Similarly, the second pupil names *'Mchele'* **(Rice)** when asked what food they ate. In Primary two, one-to-one communication was also observed as exemplified below:

26. Question	**Answer**
i) Uliletwa darasani na nani?	DS8-16: Teacher Wamaitha
Who brought you to class?	*Teacher Wamaiha*
ii) Ulikula nini leo?	CP8-16: Chai na mkate
What did you eat today?	*Tea and bread*

The phrase *'Teacher Wamaitha'* was used by DS8 to answer to the question concerning who brought her to class. Likewise, the phrase *'Chai na mkate'* **(Tea and bread)** entailing coordination is used to respond to the question pertaining to what they ate that morning. In Primary three class, the teacher and the pupils engaged in the following interactive process:

27. Question	**Answer**
i) Habari?	DS9-16: Mzuri
How are you?	*Fine*
ii) Where is your father?	CP9-16: At home

The teacher's greeting is responded to using the word *'Mzuri'* **(Fine)** while the phrase, **'at home'** answers the inquiry about where the pupil's father is. It was observed that the interactive process called for constant conversation between children with mental handicap and neurological impairment as accessed in this study, and with teachers, caregivers among others. The teachers pointed out that personal interaction create a feeling of being appreciated in the children and builds confidence in them to speak. On seeing the teachers speak, the children also feel encouraged to speak and this aides in learning components of speech. Hassold and Patterson (1998) note that the basis for communication is social interaction and certain conversational skills such as turn-taking can be developed at a very young age.

4.3.2   Imitation

This study established that another speech technique used by teachers involved imitation. This was achieved by the teachers asking the pupils to repeat sounds, words or simple poems and songs after them. This study established that the technique was used in four out of the five classes. The teacher in Primary one class for instance, involved her class in reciting the following nursery rhyme:

Jonnie x2

Yes papa

Eating sugar

No papa

Telling lies

No papa

Open your mouth

Aaah aah aah

Close your mouth

Mmh mmh mmh.

The teacher pointed out that in reciting the rhyme above, the children unknowingly practiced the articulation of the bilabial plosive / p / as in **'papa'** and **'open'** and the bilabial nasal / m / as in **'mouth'** and **'mmh'**. It can be inferred that the rhyme is chosen according to sounds first acquired by children. This is in line with what studies say. According to Ingram (1976), the voiceless bilabial plosive / p / and the bilabial nasal / m / are acquired first in speech development and that explains the choice of this poem. The teachers indicated that reciting poems and singing is a technique popular among children with DS and CP. It gives positive results, however long it takes. Sound play, calling for repetition of sounds the children can produce, gives them a feeling of accomplishment in the early stages of speech training. The study observed that imitation as a speech technique created great interest in the children to learn to speak. The element of pupils aspiring to imitate how they were taught was a more motivating method that not only ensured full participation, but also instilled a sense of fulfillment in the pupils having achieved what the teachers had done. This reinforces Drew and Hardman's (2000) view that education should present an environment that stimulates development of maximum potential.

4.3.3   Use of real objects

The use of real objects as a speech technique was observed in all the five classes used in this study. This involved showing the pupils objects within the classroom and asking them to name them. The teachers indicated that they use the technique to mainly teach vocabulary. In the nursery class for instance, the following interactive process using real objects was used in order to initiate speech and build vocabulary in the children:

28. Question	Answer
i) Hii ni nini? (Pointing at a towel)	DS1-12: Towel
What is this?	*A towel*
ii) Hii ni nini? (Pointing at a basin)	CP1-9: Karai
What is this	*Basin*

The pupils were shown a towel and basin in class which they named appropriately, as *'Towel'* and *'Karai'* **(Basin).** In the pre-primary class, the teacher posed questions and the following responses were given:

29. Question	Answer
i) What is this? *(Touching a table)*	DS4-10: Table
ii) What is this? *(Touching a chair)*	CP4-12: Chair

A table and chair shown to the pupils by the teacher were correctly named. The teacher in primary one class also used real objects for vocabulary building among the children as exemplified below:

30. Question   **Answer**

i) Hii ni nini? *(Holding a ruler)*   DS6-13: Ruler

What is this?

ii) Hii ni nini? *(Touching a chair)*   CP7-13: Kiti

What is this?   *Chair*

The pupils in this class were asked to name a ruler and a chair which they correctly did. The teacher in Primary two class also used real objects to teach vocabulary to the pupils in her class. Random questions posed gave rise to the following responses:

31. Question   **Answer**

i) Hii ni nini? *(Pointing at a radio)*   DS8-16: Radio

What is this?   *Radio*

ii) What is this *(Holding a duster)*   CP8-16: Duster

The teacher showed the pupils a radio and a duster which they correctly named. The teachers contend that real objects, especially those around the learner, help to contextualize language and make understanding easy for children such as those this study focuses on. They therefore use objects in class to sharpen speech perception skills, which leads to speech development (Ndung'u, 2009: Personal Interview). This is in line with what the Kenya Ministry of Education (1995) suggests and which is cited by Kiarie (2006). It recommends the use of concrete materials as much as possible to promote understanding of concepts in especially, children with mental handicap. It also affirms what is stated by Piaget (1969) in the Theory of Cognitive Development concerning a child's cognitive capacities and how they unfold. Children must experience and understand a phenomenon actively in the real world before they are able to put the event into words and demonstrate the mastery of the problem. The study observed that the use of objects provided this kind of environment for the children accessed in this study and helped their speech to grow.

4.3.4 Pictures and Drawings

This study also observed that teachers use pictures and drawings to help the children develop and produce speech. The use of this speech technique was observed in three of the five classes accessed in this study. In the Nursery class, the teacher showed the pupils pictures and drawings and posed question which realized the following responses:

33. Question	Answer
i) Hii ni nini? *(Pointing at a picture of a balloon)*	DS1-12: Balloon
What is this?	*Balloon*
ii) Hii ni nini? *(Pointing at a picture of a doll)*	CP1-9: Mtoto
What is this?	*A child (doll)*

The teacher in the pre-primary class also posed the following questions based on pictures and drawings displayed in class and got responses from the pupils:

34. Question	Answer
i) Hii ni shape gani? *(Pointing at a drawing of a circle)*	DS4-10: Circle
What shape is this one?	*Circle*
ii) Hii ni rangi gani? *(Pointing at colour blue)*	CP4-12: Blue
Which colour is this?	*Blue*

In primary one class, the question and response below were realized using the same speech technique:

35. Question	Answer
i) Hii ni nini? *(Showing the picture of a handbag)*	DS7-12: Mfuko

What is this?   *Handbag*

According to the teachers, the need to speak builds up in the children when they focus on pictures or drawings. They benefit from communication devices that allow them to point at things in order to make their desires known. This affirms what Dockrell and Messer (1999) state that pictures help with communication since they provide the child with rudimentary tools to express their needs. That mental development progresses as a result of children's interactions with the surrounding. This is also in agreement with what the Kenya Ministry of Education (1995) recommends and which is cited by Kiarie (2006). It states that visual materials should be used extensively to promote understanding of concepts by children with mental handicap. The study noted that the use of pictures and drawings promoted positive growth of speech in both children with DS and CP.

Summary of techniques used in speech development

It was observed that techniques used cut across all the classes. However, their frequency of use in each class was dependant upon their popularity in that class and availability of teaching aids. Nevertheless, of the most commonly used methods of developing speech in children with DS and CP, communication on one-to-one and use of objects were the most applied, in all the five classes accessed by this study (100%). The other two methods discussed in this study stood at 80% both. The percentages were determined by looking at the frequency of occurrence for each technique in the five classes. For instance, Imitation was not observed in Primary three class. The teacher attributed this to the age of the learners. Having achieved linguistic milestone, they frowned upon being told to repeat every word after the teacher and instead, preferred making their own effort. On the other hand, this study observed that pictures and drawings were not put into use in Primary two class. It was noted that teaching aids that would facilitate the use of this method were scarce in the class, probably due to lack of effort on the part of the teacher.

Nevertheless, the teachers interviewed reiterated that the techniques are complementary and are used in a complementary manner. They stated that as much as there is notable success in speech training, it is not possible to single out a specific technique as playing a superior role to the rest. A variety of techniques (three to four) are brought into play in order to achieve maximum results (Wanjiru and Mwangi, 2009: Personal Interview). This affirms what Kumin (1994) says that speech and Language treatment is complex and can include different approaches, a variety of goals and many different activities. They assert that the goal is to find approaches and methods which will enable each child to reach his/her communication potential. Whatever little milestones they make in speech training, they consider it a great success.

Going by the discussion of the study data on complete structures in section 4.1, it can be inferred that the methods used go a long way in promoting speech. The desire to speak intensifies through communication on one-to-one, imitation, use of real objects among others. In the process, the learners develop vocabulary and consequently, adequate speech. This affirms Molloy's (1965) view that in teaching trainable children to talk, the goal must be good usable speech and not useful speech. If they are able to communicate their basic needs, that will be termed successful, bearing in mind their handicapping conditions.

Summary of the chapter

In this chapter, data from the respondents was analysed. The speech ability of children with DS and CP at the time of this study was discussed and the relationship between their CA and speech development presented. The techniques used to enhance speech were also identified and discussed. In the next chapter, we cover the findings and give recommendations. Suggestion for further related research is also given.

CHAPTER FIVE

SUMMARY OF FINDINGS, CONCLUSION AND RECOMMENDATIONS

5.1 Introduction

In the previous chapter, the study data was presented and analysed. This data was discussed with the help of three theories. This chapter provides the summary of the findings of this study. It also provides a conclusion derived from the summary as well as recommendations not only for further research, but also for what the study felt needed to be done to enhance the whole concept of speech development in children with DS or CP.

5.2 Summary and findings

The first objective focused on the speech ability of children with DS and CP at the time of this study. According to Blodgett (2006), mental retardation is the most common cause of delayed speech or defective speech in both articulation and in structure. Similarly, children with CP also experience speech problems and motor coordination difficulties (Honda, 2006). Though the scope of this study did not cover aspects of possible brain damage in relation to speech development in children with DS and CP accessed, it established useful information with regard to speech ability, effect of chronological age and methodology in teaching speech to these children.

It emerged that although DS is mental and CP is largely neurological, both have the same effect on these children as far as speech development and patterns are concerned. In both cases, the pupils show the use of both defective and complete structures. The frequency of this mix of structures is higher in the lower classes but reduces as the children move to higher classes. One major problem noted was the inability to construct long sentences. A significant 15 out of 20 respondents (75%) could not manage long sentences. Instead, it was noted that most of the responses were made up of short sentences constructed upon prompting. As observed in the discussions, professional view (Hodge & William, 1999; Dockrell & Messer, 1999) points to undeveloped motor system in the speech center in the brain, which affects reflexes and centrally generated motor commands, therefore inhibiting ability for long sentences.

The study established that these children showed a disparity in the use of imperative, interrogative and declarative clauses. The fact that most of those accessed had a high frequency of declarative clauses, common with mentally sound cases, showed that despite the conditions of DS and CP, these children were able to make speech structures just like people with normal speech.

Nevertheless, this study observed that although there were instances of conditional ellipses, omission, substitution and insertion that define the defective speech of children with DS and CP, they are still able to communicate semantically. This occurs through prompting, imitation or when triggered by a need to express views among themselves during play. This study therefore noted that although DS is mental and CP is neurological, the speech patterns are basically the same though it was initially thought they would be different. However, the findings of this study showed that children with CP had lower percentages of complete structures compared to children with DS, despite the fact that the latter are known to have a higher prevalence of mental retardation. The study thus feels there is need for in depth research to get the specific differences between the two.

The second objective set out to describe and analyse the relationship between the age of these children and their speech development. This study observed that growth in speech was due to among other things, maturity and the communication needs that emerge. It was noted that children with DS and CP were more likely to have more defective structures at a younger age and at lower levels of schooling. Comparatively, respondents of below 11 years of age had more defective structures in their speech than their counterparts of 13 years and above. In relation to this, children in lower levels of learning (Nursery) had not overcome defective elements of speech. This changed as they moved through to higher levels of Primary. There is a remarkable reduction of defective structures in the higher classes. However, due to certain physiological growth inhibitions especially on the brain limits in children with DS and poor motor coordination related to muscles responsible for speech production in children with CP, the capacity to achieve complete speech like other normally developing children is inhibited. Dancie (2009) states that in children with CP, damage to the neuromuscular sites involved in the execution of speech movements may affect strength and timing of muscle contraction. However, the study observed that respondent CP1, CP7, CP8 and CP9 displayed fairly complete and coherent speech as compared to their counterparts. There was need therefore, to place them in regular schools under inclusive education as recommended in Salamanca Statement and Framework for Action during the UN convention (Ref: Chapter one, p.1), and not with children with MR.

The third objective aimed at evaluating the intervention techniques used to enable children with DS and CP develop speech. Kumin (1994) postulates that speech and Language treatment is complex and can include different approaches, a variety of goals and many different activities. The study established that a variety of complementary techniques to help correct the situation are in application within the special schools curriculum. They include learning speech through imitation, one-on-one communication between instructors and pupils, use of real objects and use of pictures and drawings. The study observed that the mental handicap or neurological impairment does not for instance; affect the children's knowledge of objects which they identify correctly any time they are pointed at by the teacher in class. They are also able to communicate, though with slight defects, among themselves during play or with their teachers. The findings of this study indicate that through these activities, the children's speech perception skills are awakened and they ultimately learn how to speak.

This study further noted that the intervention techniques used cut across all the classes. However, their frequency of use in each class was dependant upon their popularity in that class and the availability of teaching aids. For instance, the use of objects was common at the beginners level, imitation at the middle level and communication on one-to-one at the terminal level. However, the most commonly used intervention techniques involved communication on one-to-one and use of objects, observed in all the five classes. The teachers found the aspect of an active communication with the pupils having an immediate feedback and it was possible to evaluate whether the children had mastered a concept of speech or not. The use of concrete materials promoted understanding of concepts in the children. Their ability to experience and understand a phenomenon actively in the real world made it possible for them to put it in words.

5.3 Conclusion

Based on the findings given above, this study concluded that though DS and CP affected speech development, they did not necessarily hinder meaningful communication. All it requires are concerted efforts through appropriate techniques to minimize cases of ellipsis and other defective structures in the speech of children with DS and CP. However, it may be concluded that these children find the use of short sentences and one-word sentences an effortless exercise. Long sentences are a major challenge due to developmental challenges in speech centers of the brain.

It can be concluded that class level and mental age become factors that shape speech development to perfection, since speech gets better as the child moves to higher levels of primary. This is commensurate with intensified intervention techniques. However, the study noted that most children in the target group have a higher CA as opposed to their MA.

It may also be concluded in this study that speech ability develops with chronological age. There will be more cases of inability of complete structures at the lower levels of learning, but it is a problem that reduces as they rise through to the higher levels of schooling. This study therefore finds that continued interaction within a school environment, coupled with brain development that comes with age, minimizes the speech problems earlier experienced at nursery level. The more children with DS and CP remain under structured instruction, the more they develop ability to overcome their deficiencies and are therefore able to communicate meaningfully. Though the possibility of total lack of speech development has been studied and confirmed to exist, this study concluded that it is rare given that one out of the twenty respondents exhibited it.

5.4 Recommendations

On the basis of the findings and conclusions emerging from this study, the following recommendations have been made:

1. Children with DS and CP have the ability to develop speech despite their handicapping conditions. They should therefore be supported to make use of useful speech to communicate their basic needs. Cases of omission, substitution and insertion in their speech do not act as a hindrance to their ability to communicate. There is also need to observe inclusive education especially for those children with purely neurological impairment and whose level of speech is advanced. For instance, respondent CP1, CP7, CP8 and CP9 should be enrolled in a regular school.

2. From the findings, it is obvious that speech improves with the advancement in age and class level. This study therefore recommends that teachers should adopt speech techniques that give maximum results for each age group and class level of children with DS and CP. The younger the child and the lower his/her class level, the more patience expected from the teachers.

3. In the Theory of Cognitive Development it is stated that a child's cognitive capacities unfold naturally, although the influence of the environment is substantial. This study

calls for a collaborative approach among all stakeholders in assisting children with DS and CP develop speech. The teachers should therefore bring into play a variety of techniques in order to ensure maximum results in speech development. Policy makers and curriculum developers should provide special schools with adequate teaching aids that provide a suitable environment for speech development in children with DS and CP.

5.5   Suggestions for further study

The following have been suggested as possible areas for further research:

1. This study only focused on speech development in children with DS and CP. Since these are not the only children with speech problems, it would be necessary to also look at speech development in children with Autism.

2. Research should also be carried out on the role of parents in the development of speech in children with DS and CP.

BIBLIOGRAPHY

Ainsworth, P. & Baker, P. C. (2004). *Mental Retardation-A resource for parents, caregivers and counselors*. USA: American University Press.

Anderson, V & Newby, H. (1973). *Improving the child's speech*. New York: Oxford University press.

Beirne- Smith, M. Patton, J. & Kim, S. (2006). *An introduction to Intellectual disabilities* (7th ed). New Jersey: Pearson Prentice Hall.

Bjorklund, R. (2007). *Cerebral palsy*. New York: Marshall Cavendish Corporation.

Blodgett, H.E.(2006). Mentally Retarded Children-what parents and others should know. USA: University of Minnesota Press.

Bloodstein, O. (1984). *Speech Pathology-An Introduction*. USA: Houghton Mifflin Company.

Bowen, C. (1998). Speech and Language Development in Infants and young Children-A practical guide for family and teachers. Melbourne: Ecer Press.

Buckley, S. & Bird, G. (2001). Speech and language development for children with Down syndrome. UK: The Down syndrome Education Trust.

Cantwell, D. & Baker, L. (1987) *Developmental speech and language disorder.* New York: The Guilford press.

Caruso, A.J. & Strand, E. (1999). *Clinical management of motor speech disorders in children.* New York: Hamilton Printing Company.

Cicchetti, D. & Beeghly, M. (1990). *Children with Down syndrome-A developmental perspective.* UK: Cambridge University Press.

Crane, L. (2002*). Mental Retardation- A community integration approach.* USA: Thomson Learning Inc.

Dancie, J. (October 18th, 2009) *Journal on speech development in children with cerebral palsy.*

Dockrell, J. & Messer, D. (1999). *Children's language and Communication Difficulties- Understanding identification and intervention.* Cornwall: TJ International Ltd.

Drew, C. & Hardman, M. (2000). *Mental Retardation-A life cycle approach.* New Jersey: Prentice Hall Inc.

Elsenson, J & Ogilvie, M. (1963*). Speech Correction the Schools (2nd ed).* New York: The Macmillan Company.

Finnie, N. R. (2004). *Handling the young children with cerebral palsy at home (3rd ed).* UK: Butterworth Heinemann.

Gammon, C.S. (2001). *Down syndrome phonology: Developmental patterns and Intervention strategies.* USA: University of Washington.

Halliday, M.A.K. (1985). *An Introduction to Functional Grammar.* London: A division of Hodder and Stoughton.

Hassold, T. J. & Patterson, D. (1998*). Down syndrome: A Promising Future Together.* UK: Wiley-Liss Inc.

Heward, W. L. (1996). *Exceptional children- An introduction to Special Education. (5th ed).* New Jersey: Pearson education. Inc.

Hinchcliffe, A. (2007). *Children with cerebral palsy-A Manual for Therapists, Parents and Community Worker*s. London: Sage Publications Inc.

Honda, W. L. (2006). *Journal of the Acoustical Society of Japan:* "Task Planning Mechanism of speech motor control". Japan Science Technology Corporation, CREST Project(Vol. 56, No. 11; p.771).

Ianneli, V. (March 26th, 2005) *Down syndrome Fact-Journal on Paediatric Basics.* New York Times Company, available online at http//pediatrics.about.com/od/weeklyquestion/a/05-gen-syndroms.htm

Journal of National Institute on Deafness and other Communication Disorders.
April, 2001; No. 00-4781. Bethesda: NIH Publication, available online at
http://www.nidcd.nih.gov/health/voice/speechandlanguage.html

Journal of National Institute on Deafness and other Communication Disorders
October 2002, available online at http://en.wikipedia.org/wiki/ accessed on 9/9/2010.

Kiarie, M (2006) *Educational services for students with Mental Retardation in
Kenya.* International Journal of Special Education; Southern Connecticut State
University. Vol 21, No. 2.

Kombo, D. & Tromp, D. (2006*). Proposal and Thesis writing - An introduction.*
Nairobi: Pauline's publications Africa.

Kumin, L. (1994). *Intelligibility of speech in children with Down's syndrome in
natural settings; parents' perspective, perceptual and motor skills,* available online at
hhtp//www.downs-syndrome.org/information/language.

Ladefoged, P. (1982*). A Course in Phonetics* (2nd edition). New York: Harcourt
Brace Jovanorich Publishers.

Leung, A. K. & Kao, C. P. (June, 1999). *American Family Physician Journal on
Evaluation and Management of the child with Speech Delay,* available online at
http://www.med.umich.edu/yourchild/topics/speech.htm, 59(110:3121-8, 3135.

Levitt, S. (2010). *Treatment of Cerebral Palsy and Motor delay (5ᵗʰ edition)*.
London: John Wiley and Sons Ltd.

Maneno, J. & Runo, M. (2007). *Introduction to Speech and Language Disorders in Children with Learning Disabilitie*s. Nairobi: Department of Special Education.

Masakhwe, P. (2009). *Even top schools do not have room for disabled children*.
The   Saturday Standard 24ᵗʰ January. P. 7

Massamba, D. P. M. (1996). *Phonological Theory: History and Development*. Dar
es Salaam: Dar es Salaam University Press.

Mathooko, P.M & Mudhune, E. S (February 27ᵗʰ-28ᵗʰ, 2004). "Marekebisho yaa
mitalaa ya ufundishaji sarufi: Mathalani Ngeli za Nomino za Kiswahili". *Karatasi lililowakilishwa katika* kongamano *juu ya marekebisho ya mitalaa ya Kiswahili nchini Kenya*. Kenyatta University.

Mbaabu, I. (1992). *Sarufi ya Kiswahili*. Nairobi: Information handbook.

McBrayer, K. F. & Lian, M. J. (2002). *Special Needs Education-Children with Exceptionalities*. China: The Chinese University Press.

Ministry of Education Science and Technology (1994). Education in Kenya:
Information Handbook.

Ministry of Education Science and Technology (August, 2004). *Development of Education in Kenya.* August, 2004.

Molloy, J. S. (1965). *Teaching the retarded child to talk- A guide for parents and teachers.* London: University of London press Ltd.

Mugenda, A. B. (2008) *Social Sciences-Theory and Principles.* Nairobi: Arts press.

Mutai, B.K (2000*). How to write quality Research Proposal: A complete and simplified_Recipe.* New York: Thelley publications.

Mutua, D. M & Dimitrov, N.K (2001). *The journal of speech education.* "Parents' expectations about future outcomes of children with mental retardation in Kenya: Differential effects of gender and severity of MR". Pg.35, 172-180.

Ndung'u, R. W. (1991). *The Acquisition of Gikuyu Syntactic Structures by Gikuyu Children aged between 3 and 5 years.* Unpublished M. A. Thesis: Kenyatta University.

Ndurumo, M.M (1993*). Exceptional Children- Developmental Consequences and Interventions.* Nairobi: Longman Kenya Ltd.

Ngigi, A. & Macharia, D. (2006*). Education Policy Overview Paper.* Kenya: IT Power East Africa. May, 2006.

Nyamasyo, E. (1985*). Acquisition of Syntax by a four year old child.* Unpublished
M.A. Thesis: University of Nairobi.

Oelwein, P.L. (1995). *Teaching reading to Children with Down syndrome-A guide
for parents and teachers.* USA: Woobine House.

Okumu, N. (2006). Tathmini ya mpangilio wa kisintaksia wa ngeli za nomino za
Kiswahili. Ufunzaji katika shule za Nairobi. Unpublished M.A. Thesis. Kenyatta
University.

Orodho, J.A. (2004). *Techniques of writing Research Proposals and Reports in
Education and Social Sciences.* Nairobi: Reata printers.

Oswago, J.A. (2005). *Lexical density of the spoken language of MHC- A case
study of Jacaranda school; Nairobi._* Unpublished M.A Dissertation;   Kenyatta
University.

Peacock, J. (2000). *Cerebral Palsy-Perspectives on Disease and Illnes*s. USA:
Capstone Press.

Piaget, J. (1969). *Stages in cognitive development,* available online at
http./tip.psychology.org/piaget.html

Plante, E. & Beeson, M. (2004). *Communication and Communication Disorders-
A Clinical Introduction.* New York: Pearson Education Inc.

Pruthi, G. (1994). *Language Development in children with Mental Retardation.* National Council of Educational Research and Training.

Rondal, J. A. (1995*). Exceptional language development in Down syndrome- Implications for the cognition-language relationship.* New York: The Press Syndicate of the University of Cambridge.

Republic of Kenya (1995). *Education in Kenya: Information Handbook.* Nairobi: Government Printers.

Republic of Kenya (2009). *Ministry of Education- Special Needs Education Policy.* Nairobi: Government Printers.

Reynolds, T. & Dombeck, M. (August 24th, 2006). *Journal on Mental Retardation-Intellectual Disabilities.* "Useful methods for Teaching Mentally Retarded Students", available online at www.mentalhelp.net/poc/view-doc.php%3,10365

Selikowitz, M. (1997). *Down syndrome-the fact (2nd ed).* New York: Oxford University Press.

Schoenstadt, A. (June 27th, 2006). *Journal on Language Development in Autistic Children.* "Understanding Normal Development", available online at http://autism.emedtv.com/autism/language-development-in-autistic-children.html.

Schwartz, S. M. (1996). *The New Language of Toys: Teaching Communication*

Skills to Special Needs Children. Bethesda: Woodbine House.

Shriver, E. K. (March 24th, 2010). *Journal on National Institute of Health and Human Development,* available online at http://online library.wiley.com/doi/10.1002/neu.20237/abstract.

Sulkes, S. B. (October, 2006) *The Merck Manuals online Medical Library.*

Westling, D.L. (1986). *Introduction to Mental Retardation.* New Jersey: Prentice Hall Inc.

Zattore, R. J. & Gandour, J. T. (March 12th, 2008). *Journal on Neural Specialization for Speech and Pitch.* "Moving beyond the dichotomies". Phil Trans R Soc B, available online ukpmc.ac.uk/abstract/MED/17890, 363(1493):1087-104,3Bj.

APPENDICES

APPENDIX A1

RESEARCH INSTRUMENTS

Sample interview guide for teachers of children with DS and CP.

Instructions

A study is being carried out to find out what strategies are employed by teachers at Maria Magdalena Special School for Mentally Handicapped Children to facilitate speech development among children with DS and CP. The study seeks to establish the extent to which these strategies enhance speech development among these children. The findings of this study will be useful to both parents of such children and policy makers in the special education sector.

Your cooperation during this exercise will be greatly appreciated and your responses to the questions will be kept confidential.

1. What is your name?

2. For how long have you taught in this school?
   a) Less than 1 year.
   b) Between 1 and 5 years
   c) Between 5 and 10 years
   d) Over 10 years

3. Are you specially trained to take care of children with DS and CP?

4. What category of class are you in charge of?

5. How many of your learners suffer from:

   a) Down syndrome

   b) Cerebral palsy

6. For each of the learners in (5) above, what are their chronological ages and the year of admission to the school?

7. How would you describe the speech ability of the children with DS and CP sampled?

8. Among the children with CP, how many suffer from mental handicap?

9. Describe the techniques you use in order to assist those without or with minimal speech develop it.

10. Which techniques are popular in your class?

11. To what degree would you consider specific techniques used effective? (Give examples of linguistic milestones achieved by each sampled child in your class).

OBSERVATION CHECKLIST

Classroom chart recording linguistic output of children observed.

Respondent	Age	linguistic output
Sounds		
Words		
Sentences		

APPENDIX A2

BACKGROUND INFORMATION ON CHILDREN WITH DS AND CP NURSERY CLASS

Respondent DS1

Age: 12 years

Year admitted: 2006 when she was eight years old

Condition: DS

Diagnosis: Detected at birth

Speech ability: Joined   nursery class with minimal speech which has
                    since advanced. Speech disconnected.

Respondent CP1

Age: 9 Years

Year admitted: 2007 at the age of seven years

Condition: CP

Diagnosis: Detected at six months after undergoing an operation due to
                    intestinal obstruction.

Speech ability: Improved from minimal to adequate

Respondent DS2

Age: 11 years

Year admitted: 2006 at age of 8year.

Conditions: DS

Speech ability: Utters one or two words only.

Respondent DS3

Age: 9year

Year admitted: 2007 at age of seven.

Condition: DS coupled with poor eye sight.

Speech ability: Has improved from being mute to cooking and babbling.

Respondent CP2

Age: 9years

Condition: 2007 at age of seven

Condition: Combination of CP and MR

Speech ability: Improved from being mute to cooing and uttering two to three words.

Respondent CP3

Age: 11years

Year admitted: 2008 at age ten

Condition: CP

Diagnosis: Detected at birth

Speech ability: Uses disconnected speech.

PRE- PRIMARY

Respondent DS4

Age: 10years

Year admitted: 2007 at age eight.

Condition: DS

Diagnosis: Detected at birth

Development: Began his schooling in a regular school then moved to special school.

Speech ability: Improved from minimal and incomprehensible to adequate though it is largely disconnected.

Respondent DS5

Age: 11years

Year admitted: 2006 at age seven

Condition: DS

Diagnosis: detected at birth.

Speech ability: Minimal and characterized with omissions and substitution.

Respondent CP4

Age: 12years

Year admitted: 2007 at age ten

Condition: CP

Diagnosis: Detected at birth

Speech ability: Improved from minimal to advanced.

Respondent CP5

Age: 13years

Year admitted: 2006 at age ten

Condition: CP. Also suffers from constant throat infections

Diagnosis: Detected at birth.

Speech ability: Adequate though characterized with substitution

PRIMARY ONE

Respondent DS6

Age:	13 years
Year admitted:	2007 at age eleven
Condition:	DS
Speech ability:	Has complete speech.

Respondent CP6

Age:	13years
Year admitted:	2004 at age eight
Condition:	Combination of CP and MR.
Diagnosis:	Detected at birth.
Speech ability:	Improved from minimal to adequate.

Respondent DS7

Age:	12 years
Year admitted:	2006 at age nine.
Condition:	DS
Speech ability:	Improved from mute to minimal.

Respondent CP7

Age:	13 years
Year admitted:	2007 at age eleven
Condition:	CP
Diagnosis:	Detected at birth.
Development:	Began his schooling in a regular school before moving to a

special one.

Speech ability: Has slurred but advanced speech. Able to use long sentences.

PRIMARY TWO
Respondent DS8

Age   16years

Year admitted: 2007 at age fourteen.

Condition: DS

Diagnosis: Detected at birth.

Speech ability: Has complete speech with a few cases of omission.

Respondent CP8

Age: 16years

Year admitted: 2001 at age nine

Condition: CP

Diagnosis: Detected at birth

Speech ability: Improved from minimal to advanced.

PRIMARY THREE
Respondent DS9

Age: 16years

Year admitted: 2003 at age nine

Condition: DS

Diagnosis: Detected at birth

Speech ability: Improved from minimal to adequate.

Respondent CP9

Age:	15years
Year admitted:	2005 at age eleven
Condition:	CP
Diagnosis:	Detected at birth
Speech ability:	Improved from minimal to adequate.

Respondent CP10

Age:	16years
Year admitted:	2001 at age seven
Condition:	Combination of CP and MR.
Diagnosis:	Detected at birth
Speech ability:	Improved from mute to use of disconnected speech.

Respondent DS10

Age:	16 years
Year admitted	2004 at age ten
Condition:	DS
Diagnosis:	Detected at birth
Speech ability:	Improved from minimal to adequate.

APPENDIX A3

LINGUISTIC OUTPUT OF CHILDREN OBSERVED AND RECORDED USING A TAPE RECORDER AND AN OBSERVATION CHECKLIST

Respondent	Age	Gender	Linguistic Output	
			Defective Structures	Complete Structures
DS1 Nursery	12	Girl	Sausaseg= Sausage	Simsim
			Mamba=namba (number)	Soda
				Ni mimi
			Disa= Dirisha	Sweet
			Kakakati=yoghurt	Biskuti
			Chubuni=sabuni	Makono
			Bababati=chapatti	Baridi
			Watototo=watoto	Maji moto
			Ng'eno=meno	Balloon
			Pena=mapema	Saloon
			Collogate=colgate	Nywele
			Mombe=ng'ombe	Mchele
				Nyama
				Ndengu
				Cake
				Towel
				Ticha
				Karai
				Mum=mother

				Smart
				Macho
				Sikio
				Pua
				Anapika
DS2 Nursery	11	Boy	Nil	leta yangu
DS3 Nursery	9	Boy	Nil	Nil
DS4 Pre-primary	10	Boy	Saki=sitaki Bulack=black adako=triangle ed=red Pre=present Sha = Shapes	Nje Class Table Kiti Teacher Eyes Mouth Blue Circle
DS5 Pre-primary	11	Boy	tention=Attention Mombe=ng'ombe	At ease Chair Teacher Mouth
DS6 Primary	13	Boy		Bendera Ruler

one				Duka
				Soko
				Bag
				Mfuko=handbag
				Ruai
				Kung'oa mawe
				Kupika
				Homa ya nguruwe
DS7 Primary one	12	Girl		Door
				Dirisha
				Duka
				Mfuko=handbag
				Letter
				Fit(Response to greeting)
				Adam Ng'ang'a
				Kinoo
				Unatoka wapi?
DS8 Primary two	16	Girl	Mu Esther=Mwalimu Esther	Red
				Damu
				Ya kusoma
				Kumi
				Teacher Wamaitha
				Makasi
				Ya kukata
				Mbili
				Redio

DS9 Primary three	16	Boy		Mzuri
				Kule
				Chapati
				Ya mwalimu
				Huko
				Karatasi
				Viatu
				Sharti
				Yangu
				Shingo
				Biro
				Simu
				Chupa
				Kofia
				Table
				Chair
DS10 Primary three	16	Girl		Catholic
				Gatanga
				Table
				Dress
				Ndoo
				Egg
				Simu
				Doll
				Book
				Shingo

				Head
				Mkono
				Masikio
				Ear
				Redio
				Mahindi
				Kitambaa
				Tumeshukuru
				Mkate
				Sausage
				Biscuit
				Homa ya nguruwe huletwa na?
				Tutaenda lini mid-term?
				Kusalimia mama
CP1 Nursery	9	Girl		Number
				Karai
				Mtoto
				Kuwekelea mtoto
				Maji
				Kwa tap
				Taulo
				Sabuni
				Teacher
				Anaakisha
				'Anapoa' for 'Anazima'

				Smart
				Mzuri
				Dirisha
				Nyamazeni tuombe
				Mimi nilijifunza
				Tunakula
				Tutalala
				Tubadilishe nguo
				Mchele
CP2 Nursery	9	Boy	Ba=Baba	Nipe Teacher
CP3 Nursery	11	Girl	Nyuni=sabuni Kayi=karayi Mama=nyama Ta=mafuta Mart=smart Nyeku=ndengu Seye=mchele Mpoha=mboga Pati=chapatti	Baba Nguo Nyanya Teacher
CP4 Pre-primary	12	Girl		Darasani Good morning teacher Fine thank you teacher Habari? Unaitwaje? Kwenyu ni wapi?

				Present teacher
				Shule yetu inaitwa Maria
				Magdalena
				Table
				Chair
				Shop
				Shoulder
				Eyes
				Mouth
				Blue
				White
				Circle
				Red
				Triangle
				Hii ni nini?
CP5 Pre-primary	13	Girl	Kable=table Kair=chair Kika=teacher It is a gok=It is a dog Whike=white Gak=black Chako=circle Guster=duster Heag=head Shoga=shoulder Mout=mouth	Hair Eyes

			Geen = Green Ng'ek=red Shek=Shapes Mamba=number	
CP6 Primary one	13	Girl	Disa-Dirisha	Kiti nyamaza amka
CP7 Primary one	13	Boy		Hii inaitwa nini? Haiwezi kuimba Inaenda polepole Yangu iko nyumbani Ni baba yangu Ameenda kazini Anapika Hii simu yako Iko hapa ndani Mama yangu yuko nyumbani Mama yangu anaweza kusoma Ni mwalimu Ndio hiyo kengele pale Mwalimu ndio alichora Ndio hiyo balloon Kiti

				Mchele
				Redio
				'Haina mawe' for 'It has no dry cells'
				Yetu iko na mawe (dry cells)
				Mbili
				Dirisha
				Baba yangu ameenda kazini
				Hii haiwezi kuimba
				Wapi?
				Ako wapi?
				'Funga hii' for 'Zima hii'
CP8 Primary two	16	Boy		Teacher
				Maria Magdalena Special School
				Chai na mkate
				Teacher Kaburu
				Colour red
				Mawili
				Number three
				Mbili
				Duster
				Chalk
				Blackboard
				Car
				Book

				Bag
				Pencil
				Boy
				Tutafunga siku gani?
				Elfu mbili na tisa
				Kuchotea ng'ombe maji
				Kuipea majani
				Kuipeleka kwa ziwa
				Redio
				Green
				Pencil
				Watakupikia mayai na chapati na kuku
CP9 Primary three	16	Boy		Fine
				My name is Francis Kimani
				Dandora
				Here
				At home
				In the dorm
				Ugali
				Cabbage
				Comb
				Jug
				Pot
				Meza
				Egg

				Simu
				Chupa
				Paper
				Book
				Doll
				Window
				Dirisha
				Bag
				Hand
				Shingo
				Redio
				Kwaheri
				Sweet
				Mahindi
				Kitambaa
				Unaitwa nani?
				Kwenyu ni wapi?
CP10 Primary one	16	Girl	mu=mwalimu Mama=nyama Ku=Wanjiku iti ooma=Kijiti cha kusoma ambaa=Kitambaa Yeye=nywele Seye=mchele twiti=switi (sweet)	Nguo Ndoo

			nsa=dirisha	
			ingo=shingo	
			Kia=masikio	
			Ma=stima	
			Yedio=redio	
			Nta=mafuta	
			Ooku=Book	

DATE DUE	RETURNED
NOV 2 0 2013	NOV 0 6 2013
NOV 2 0 2013	

CPSIA information can be obtained at www.ICGtesting.com
Printed in the USA
LVOW051358160912

298989LV00007B/44/P